Bill Mantovani

Sage 50 Accounts 2016

For users of Sage 50 Essentials, Accounts, Accounts Plus
and Accounts Professional

In easy steps is an imprint of In Easy Steps Limited
16 Hamilton Terrace · Holly Walk · Leamington Spa
Warwickshire · United Kingdom · CV32 4LY
www.ineasysteps.com

Notice of Liability
Every effort has been made to ensure that this book contains accurate
and current information. However, In Easy Steps Limited and the
author shall not be liable for any loss or damage suffered by readers
as a result of any information contained herein.

Trademarks
Sage 50® is a registered trademark of The Sage Group plc.
Microsoft® and Windows® are registered trademarks of Microsoft
Corporation. All other trademarks are acknowledged as belonging to
their respective companies.

In Easy Steps Limited supports The Forest Stewardship Council (FSC),
the leading international forest certification organisation. All our titles
that are printed on Greenpeace approved FSC certified paper carry the
FSC logo.

MIX
Paper from
responsible sources
FSC® C020837

Printed and bound in the United Kingdom

ISBN 978-1-84078-721-4

Contents

5   The Bank   57

6   Products   73

7   Invoices   87

8 Processing Sales Orders — 101

9 Purchase Orders — 109

10 Financial Reporting — 119

11 Fixed Assets — 133

1 Getting Started

This chapter takes you through the stages of preparing Sage 50 for use. It explains initial procedures for setting up Company details and various defaults required by the program.

Use the Demo data provided by Sage or Practice data (try things in a blank company) to familiarise yourself with the program at any time. Select either from File, Open or from the Select Company option at startup.

Beware

Some things, once entered, cannot be easily changed. Therefore, make sure you have all the relevant information to hand before using Sage 50 Accounts for the first time.

Introduction

Accurate accounts are vital to the efficient running of a business. If information is not entered correctly, then the accounts data will be wrong – and you can't blame the computer!

Working through Sage 50 Accounts 2016 in easy steps

This book explains in simple, easy stages how to perform the main tasks for keeping computerised business accounts. In the following chapters you are shown how to:

- Set various defaults and Company preferences

- Create customer and supplier records and set up price lists

- Set up opening balances, maintain Bank accounts

- Maintain the Nominal Ledger and run an audit trail

- Generate sales orders and control stock

- Print invoices, credit notes and statements

- Produce history and financial reports

Note: the actual functions available to you will depend on whether you have Sage 50 Accounts, Accounts Plus or Professional. You can even use this book if you work with Sage Instant Accounts.

'Preparing to start' checklist

Before getting started with Sage 50 Accounts 2016, work through the checklist below to make sure you have everything you need.

- Check the start date of your company's financial year

- Check with an accountant which VAT scheme is used

- Draw up a list of defaults to use

- Decide on users and passwords

- Back up the data if updating Sage

- Have customer, supplier and bank details to hand

- Check Product details (doing a stock take is recommended)

- Prepare a list of all opening balances

Starting Sage 50 Accounts

Turn on your computer and wait for the Windows Desktop to appear. To start your Sage 50 Accounts program, do the following:

1 Click on the Windows Start button

2 Click on All apps and scroll down to S

3 Click on the Sage Accounts folder to expand the list

4 Click on Sage 50 Accounts to start the program

5 The startup screen appears

6 Change the startup screen to one of your choice. The most common one is Customers

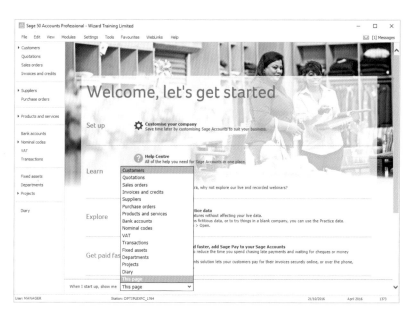

Alternatively, if a shortcut has been set up on the Windows Desktop, you can open Sage 50 by simply double-clicking on the shortcut icon:

Remember that your reporting will not be accurate until all your opening balances have been entered. Ask your accountant for these, if possible, before you start using Sage 50 Accounts.

You can create multiple delivery addresses so that you can have goods delivered to a number of customer sites, whilst specifying a different address for the invoice.

Sage 50 Desktop Views

Sage 50 Accounts lets you change how information is displayed in the Sage desktop work area. Although the options vary from module to module, typically the views may include a List display, a Process map and a Dashboard.

A typical Process map for Suppliers is shown below. You can click on an icon to jump straight to the relevant processing stage. To switch views, to List for example, do the following:

For instant help in any Sage window, simply press the F1 Help key.

1 Click on List here

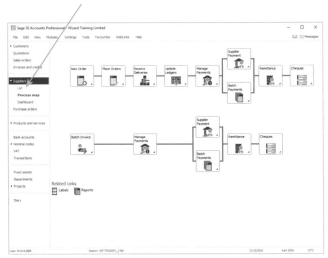

The Process map shows the workflow associated with the selected group and is a quick and convenient way of switching between related modules.

2 The Suppliers List initially shows Contact details, Balance and Credit Limit. Click here to print the list

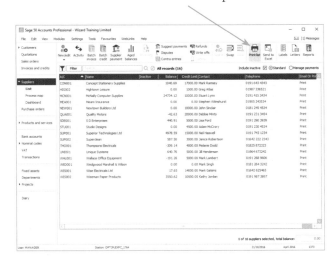

Regularly use the various Dashboard views to keep track of how your business is progressing. For example, you can quickly view your aged debtors or creditors, see which are your top customers or which items of stock are selling fast or running low.

Settings

Before Sage 50 can be used there are a number of settings and defaults that need to be entered. The rest of this chapter shows how to do this. When required, select the appropriate settings option from the following list:

1 Click on Settings on the Menu bar

2 Click on the option required

Click Help on the Sage 50 menu bar, then Shortcut Keys, to access a list of the Navigation and keyboard shortcuts.

Using Passwords

The Data Protection Act requires that any system containing confidential information, i.e. financial details etc., should be protected against unauthorised access. Sage 50 uses a password to achieve this. Once you set a password, Sage 50 always prompts you for it at startup.

As with any password, you should avoid writing it down if at all possible. Therefore, try to choose a password that is both easy for you to remember but difficult for someone else to discover. You can decrease the chance of somebody accidentally finding out your password by using a mixture of letters and numbers instead of an actual word.

1 From the Settings menu, click on Change Password

2 Type your password here

3 Repeat the password to confirm

4 Click OK to save the password

Try to avoid using obvious things like a name, phone number or car registration as a password. These are far too easy for other people to guess.

If you allocate a password to the logon name MANAGER you must ensure you never lose it, otherwise you will have to send your accounts to Sage to have the password reset.

11

Company Preferences

When you run Sage 50 for the first time, use the ActiveSetup Wizard to enter your Company details. Alternatively, or to make changes, after selecting Company Preferences from the Settings options, you can enter or edit these details as follows:

1 Enter your company name here

2 Enter your full address details

3 Complete e-mail and web addresses

4 Select VAT tab to enter VAT Ref No

5 Click OK to finish

Products and Fixed Assets Categories

After selecting Configuration from the Settings options, you can create different categories for dividing products and fixed assets for analysis:

1 Select Products tab and click on the first blank entry

2 Click Edit and enter a category name

3 Click OK

4 Click the Apply button to use

5 Repeat steps 1-4 for Fixed Assets

12

Setting up & checking Tax Codes

Sage 50 already has the standard UK and EC VAT Rates set for you together with the code T1 (standard rate – currently 20.00%) set as the default tax code. Here is a list of the codes automatically set up during installation:

- T0 – zero rated transactions
- T1 – standard rate
- T2 – exempt transactions
- T4 – sales to customers in EC*
- T7 – zero rated purchases from suppliers in EC*
- T8 – standard rated purchases from suppliers in EC*
- T9 – transactions not involving VAT

  (*Outside the UK)

There are 100 VAT codes available in Sage 50. To enter or change VAT rates, use Configuration from the Settings options:

1 Click Tax Codes tab and the required code

2 Click Edit

3 Enter the percentage rate

4 Tick if the VAT rate is for an EC Code

5 Enter Description and click OK

6 Click Apply to use

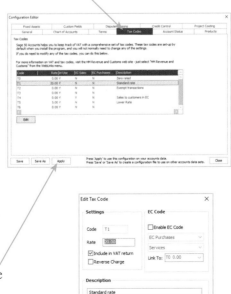

It is important to use the correct VAT codes. If you are unsure of the current UK or EU VAT rates then contact HM Revenue & Customs.

T1 is the standard UK VAT rate code.

Sage 50 uses T9 as the default tax code for all the routines that are non-vatable, e.g. journal entries, error corrections and Bank.

Don't forget

It is possible to change the Financial Year start date after you have already commenced using the program.

Hot tip

Use the Account Status facility to mark accounts which are bad debts or have exceeded their credit limit, and for placing orders on hold if necessary, etc. If you then raise an invoice, for example against an account which is a bad debt, Sage 50 will issue an on-screen warning.

...cont'd

Financial Year

The start of the financial year is entered during the installation of Sage 50 Accounts or before entering any transactions, but it is also possible to change it later:

1 From Settings on the menu bar click on Financial Year

2 To change year select the Change... button

3 Click Yes in the next two prompt windows, select the month and year and then click OK

Account Status

A useful feature within Sage 50 is that you can assign an account status to each of your accounts. You can also add an account status at any time to the 10 already set up via the Configuration Editor:

1 Click on the Account Status tab and highlight a blank line

2 Click Edit

3 Enter the Status Name

4 Tick if you want this status to place accounts 'on hold'

5 Click OK, then Apply to use

Currency & the Euro

Sage 50 is already set up with the currencies of over 30 major countries, but not the exchange rates. These details can be edited or other countries set up as required:

1 Click on Settings, Currencies and highlight the currency you want to edit, or select the first blank record to enter a new currency

2 Click Edit... to bring up the Edit Currency box

3 Enter the name of the Currency

4 Complete the Currency Code and the Currency symbol

5 Enter the Currency exchange rate

6 Enter the Major and Minor currency units

7 Click OK, then Close the Currencies box

Hot tip

When the cursor is in a numeric field, simply press F5 to access the Currency Calculator. This can be used for converting from Sterling to a Euro/Foreign Currency or to convert a Euro/Foreign Currency amount to Sterling.

Beware

Exchange rates change frequently, so make sure you have the latest rates entered before recording a foreign currency transaction. Up-to-date rates are available from a number of sources, including the internet (e.g. **www.xe.com**).

Customer & Supplier Defaults

When creating a new customer or supplier, details about credit limit, terms, discount etc. are needed. Customer and Supplier records are discussed in Chapters 2 and 3 respectively but before this, their various defaults need to be set up.

For customers, default nominal codes (N/C) start at 4000.

1 Select Customer Defaults from the Settings options

2 Enter defaults for your customer records on the first Tab

3 Click on the relevant Tabs to enter Statements, Ageing Balance and appropriate Discount defaults

A customer can be a member of a price list. However, as a customer can only belong to one price list, if you want to change the list that the selected customer belongs to, simply choose a different price list from the drop-down list. Note that on each price list, additional discounts can still be applied.

4 Click OK to save the Customer Defaults entered

5 Now, select Supplier Defaults from the Settings options

6 Enter relevant Supplier Defaults

7 Use the Ageing Tab to enter Aged Balances Period, specifying calendar months or days

Default nominal codes for suppliers start at 5000.

8 Click OK to save Supplier Defaults

16

...cont'd

Product Defaults
Defaults also need to be set up for Products:

1 Select Product Defaults from the Settings options

2 Enter the Nominal Account code here

3 Allocate the correct Tax Code for the Product

4 Complete the rest of the defaults as necessary

5 Enter the Decimal Point placing for the product

6 Click OK to save this information

Use the Finder button on the right of the Nominal Code box to speed up code entry.

Control Accounts
Sage 50 uses Control Accounts to make automatic double-entry postings to the ledger.

1 To view or edit these Nominal Codes select Control Accounts from the Settings options

2 To change a Control account click on the nominal code and type the new code or use the Finder button

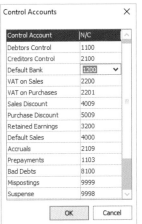

Unless you have created your own Chart of Accounts, the Control accounts should never need changing.

3 Click OK to save and close or Cancel to abandon changes

Finance Rates

Finance rates need to be set up before any credit charges can be applied to your customers.

When a Finance Charge Rate is applied to a transaction, the first rate charged will be applied monthly until the invoice is paid.

1 Select Configuration from the Settings menu and click on the Terms tab to bring up the Finance Charge Rates box

2 Click on Add to enter a new finance rate charge

You must first have set up your finance rates and the date from which they are to be applied before you can use the Charges option on the Customer toolbar.

3 Enter the date the charge is to be applied from

4 Enter the Base Rate as a percentage

5 Enter an additional charge if applicable

6 Click OK to save the new finance rate or Cancel to return to the Finance Charge Rates box

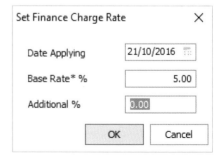

Use the Delete button on the Finance Charge Rates window to remove any unwanted charges.

7 Click Close to finish

18

2 The Customer Ledger

Learn how to use the Customer (Sales) Ledger to maintain customer records and create new ones, as well as enter credit notes and invoices. See how to view transaction activity, set up a customer price list, produce an overdue payments letter, apply credit charges and mark an invoice as disputed.

Keeping a Financial System

It is essential for all businesses to have a system to record and monitor their business and financial transactions. This information needs to be accurately recorded and kept up-to-date if it is to present a true financial position.

Such a system will involve the recording of transactions using the traditional method of bookkeeping or advanced accounting procedures, so that financial reports (i.e. profit & loss statements and balance sheet, etc.) can be produced.

These reports provide Management with information on sales, purchases, turnover, expenses, debtors and creditors, assets and liabilities, and more importantly, if the business has made a profit.

HM Revenue and Customs will also need accurate accounts, which must conform to general bookkeeping and accounting procedures. This is vital for Tax and VAT Returns. Visit the website at **www.hmrc.gov.uk** for up-to-date information on online filing and payments.

This information is also of importance to your Bank Manager, especially if there is a need to borrow money to ease cash flow problems or help set up a new business venture. Likewise, potential investors in your business may first want to see the true financial position of your accounts before making a decision.

Computerised systems have removed the majority of time consuming and repetitive tasks of manual accounting. Businesses can check their financial status on a daily basis, or over a designated period of time. This valuable information will aid important decision making and business planning and is crucial for forecasting whether a business will succeed or fail.

Sage 50 makes keeping computerised accounts easy. Many of the report templates needed are provided with the package, so producing accurate business reports is a simple matter, provided of course, that all information has been entered correctly. The following chapters guide you through the processes involved in keeping accurate and up-to-date computerised financial accounts for your business.

In keeping with most software these days, Sage makes extensive use of the internet whilst in operation, so do make sure you have an active broadband connection to make the most of the facilities.

Hot tip

Regularly monitor your Customer credit status using the Debt analysis button in the Customers toolbar. By selecting Details you can quickly see who owes you money and easily produce a handy printout of any overdue or outstanding debtors.

Debt analysis

20

The Customers Toolbar

The Customers toolbar provides features for creating customer records and viewing transaction activity, producing invoices and credit notes, marking invoices as disputed and applying credit charges. Customer Statements are produced here, plus letters, a range of reports and generating price lists.

New — Creates a new Customer Account

Edit — Opens a Customer Record

Price lists — To set up a Customer Price List

Activity — Opens Customer Activity

Aged debt — Opens Customer Aged Balances

Batch invoice — Opens the Batch Customer Invoices window

Batch credit — Opens the Batch Customer Credits window

Disputes — Opens the Disputed Items window

Credit charges — Opens the Credit Charges window

Labels — To print Customer Labels

Letters — To print Standard Letters to Customers

Statements — To print Customer Statements

Reports — To run Customer Reports

Creating Customer Records

In this window, a customer record can be added, edited or deleted. You can record agreed credit terms and even log any contact you have with a customer, such as telephone calls and who you spoke to. You can also record if invoices are sent electronically.

Hot tip

Use the New wizard for easy to follow step-by-step instructions for entering a basic new customer record.

1 Select Customers from the Sage 50 navigation bar

2 Click on a customer and use the Edit button to bring up the Customer Record window

3 Use Details to store basic customer information

4 Click the O/B button if an Opening Balance is required

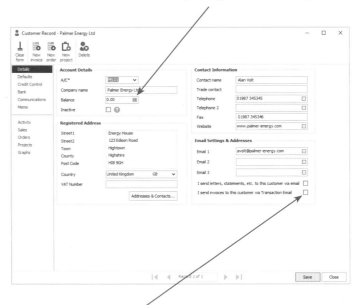

5 Tick here if invoices are sent electronically

6 Use the Credit Control option to enter any credit terms you have agreed for this customer

7 Use the Bank option to enter Bank and Payment details

8 Click Save to store the record, then Close to finish

Beware

The method of entering opening balances is different for Standard VAT and VAT Cash Accounting. Use the F1 Help key to check.

22

Viewing transactions

Once customer activity has taken place, Sage 50 offers you a variety of options for checking customer transaction details:

- View customer invoices, receipts, credit notes and balances on a monthly basis, as a graph or table.

- Use the Activity option to see a breakdown of each customer's transactions.

- View or print the customer's aged balances.

1 Open a customer record from the list and select Activity

2 Select a transaction – all items appear in the lower pane

3 Use the scroll bar to move through all the transactions

4 Click on Show to select another range of transactions, enter dates if choosing Custom Range, then click OK

Note that the following codes indicate the transaction type:

SI = Sales Invoice
SR = Sales Receipt
SC = Sales Credit
SD = Sales Discount
SP = Sales Payment
SA = Sales Payment on Account

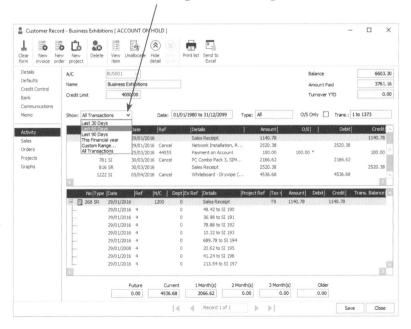

Use the Orders option to quickly view a history of the sales orders a customer has placed with you. Simply double-click on an order in the list to bring up the sales order record.

5 Click on Close to return to the Customer list

Price Lists

In Sage 50, different price lists can be set up and customers allocated to the price list of your choice. For each Price List, products can be added and different prices set up accordingly. For example, you can create custom lists for Trade, Retail, Summer or Winter Sales and Special Offers.

To create a new Price List do the following:

Hot tip

Where a selected customer is already on another price list, Sage 50 asks if you want to transfer this customer to the new list. Click Yes to transfer the customer to the new list or Yes to All to transfer all customers already on another list to the new list.

1 From the Customers toolbar click on the Price Lists button to bring up the Price Lists box

2 Click New to open the New Price List window

3 Enter Name and Description

4 Click the Add button. Select products for this list, then click Save when done

5 In the Customers section click Add to bring up a list

Hot tip

To add more than one customer at a time to your list, simply hold down the Control key and click on your selection during Step 6.

6 Select Customers

7 Click OK

8 Click Save, then Close and Close again

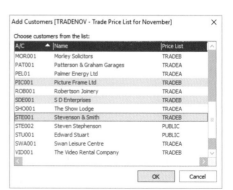

Batch Customer Invoice

Invoices are important business transaction documents and record detailed information about the goods or services supplied to the customer. Briefly, these details include the invoice number, name and address of the customer, date of sale, details of goods and/or services supplied, details of discount, total amount of money due and terms of trade.

There are different types of invoices, and Chapter 7 shows you how to create a product or a service invoice, as well as automatically creating an invoice from a sales order. However, any invoices produced manually (Batch Invoices) and sent to customers also need recording. No printout is produced.

To record a batch customer invoice do the following:

1 Choose Batch Invoice from the Customers toolbar then click here and select the customer Account Code

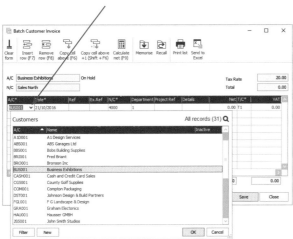

2 Change Date, Nominal Code or Department if necessary then enter the invoice number in the Ref field

3 Enter the Net value of the invoice

4 Add additional customer invoices as required

5 When finished, click Save and Yes to update the nominal ledger and customer details (details posted), then Close

Where you only know the gross value of an invoice, enter it in the Net box and use the Calculate net button (or press the F9 shortcut key) to let Sage 50 work out the correct Net value and VAT due.

Calculate net (F9)

Beware

Always check that the correct Tax Code is used (see page 13).

Batch Customer Credit Note

A credit note is used, for example, where an error is made and a customer has been overcharged on an invoice. Sometimes, damaged goods are returned and so a credit note is issued showing the amount due to the customer.

Like batch invoicing, credit notes processed manually also need to be entered. To record batch credit notes:

1 Click Batch Credit from the Customers toolbar to bring up the Batch Customer Credits window

2 Enter the customer Account Code

3 The screen displays the defaults for the nominal account code posting, VAT rate to be applied and department

Hot tip

To check the credit note has been posted, make a note of the balance for the appropriate customer in the Customers window before entering the credit note, then check that the balance has reduced by the correct amount after performing Step 6.

Don't forget

When looking at Customer activity, the transaction type (Tp) code SC indicates a Sales Credit Note.

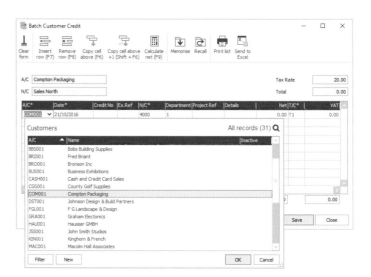

4 Enter credit details for each customer in the same way as for batch invoices

5 Check all values are correct and click Save then Yes to post the details, No to start again or Cancel to return

6 Click Close to return to the Customers window

Debtors Analysis

To identify debtors and monitor cashflow, customers' outstanding balances and transactions need to be regularly checked. These transactions are grouped by the age of the debt, either in calendar months or based on a period of days, e.g. 30, 60 and 90 days etc. Debt chasing letters can be issued if required. A business may use this information to calculate interest charges for late payment.

From the Settings menu, select Customer Defaults, then the Ageing tab to change the age of the debt from calendar months to period of days, or vice versa.

1 To view all balances, click Clear on the Customers toolbar then Aged debt to open the Aged Balances window

2 Enter the date to be used for the Aged Balances report

3 Enter the Include Payments Up To date

4 For a transaction breakdown, select a customer and click the Detailed view button on the toolbar

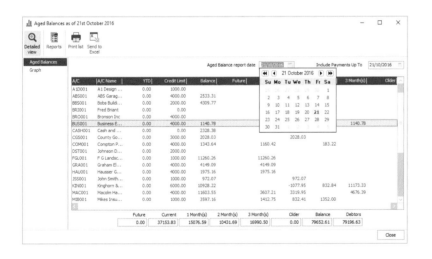

5 To see a graph format, select Graph on the navigation bar

6 To export the details to an Excel spreadsheet, simply click the Send to Excel button on the toolbar

7 Click Close to return to the Sage Desktop

Credit Control

A payment which is 30 days overdue is regarded, by default, as late. If you need to change payment terms, do the following:

1 From the Customers list window, double-click the customer you need to edit

2 Select Credit Control on the Customer Record navigation bar

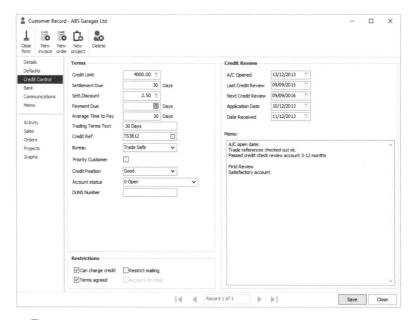

28

3 Enter new details in the Payment Due field

4 Change Average Time to Pay if necessary

5 Apply account restrictions if desired, such as placing the account on hold or allowing credit to be charged

6 Change any of the other terms as required, then click Save

7 Click Close then Close again to return to the Customers list window, and repeat these steps if you need to edit another customer

Disputed Invoices

There may be times when an invoice is questioned by the customer, so until an agreement is made the invoice can be marked as disputed. This option also applies to any invoices not fully paid. Once the problem is resolved, you can remove the disputed flag (indicator). To mark an invoice as disputed:

1 Click on the Disputes button in the Customers window

2 Use the Finder button, select a customer and then click OK

3 Click on the transaction you want to mark as disputed

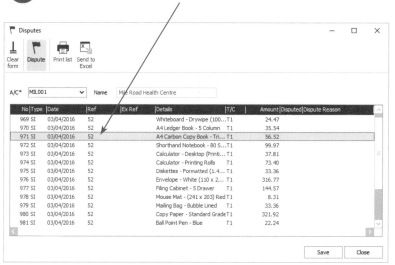

4 Click Dispute

5 Select Reason

6 Click OK

7 Note that transaction is now marked as 'd'

8 Click Save to record the disputed transaction

9 Click Close to return to the Customers list

You need to first set up Dispute Reasons using the Configuration Editor. This will then give you more accurate reporting when you need to check why an item has been marked as disputed.

The Finder button is the down-arrow on the right of a field, and becomes highlighted when you point at it.

To remove the Dispute status of an invoice, simply highlight it and click on the Dispute button again.

If you are using Standard VAT, invoices marked as disputed are still included in the VAT Return.

Customer Reports & Modem

Sage 50 provides you with a wide range of ready-designed customer reports to suit the majority of needs. To print or view a customer report, do the following:

The arrow on the right of the Customers toolbar lets you access any buttons that do not fit in the toolbar.

1 Click on the Reports button in the Customers toolbar

2 Click here on the appropriate group and select the report you require from the list

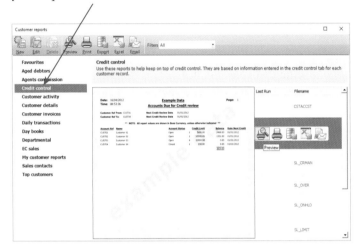

3 Place the cursor over Preview for an example of the report

4 Click the Preview or Print button to generate the report

5 After printing, Close each window

Modem

For some features, such as dialling a customer or supplier, you need to have a modem fitted in your PC. By default, the F11 key is set up by Sage 50 to open the Control Panel so that you can check if your computer has a modem installed, as follows:

If your computer modem and telephone share the same line and you have set up the Windows Phone Dialer, click on the button to the right of the telephone box in the Customer record to quickly dial the customer.

1 Press the F11 key to bring up the Windows Control Panel

2 Click on the Phone and Modem icon

3 Select the Modems tab to see if a modem is fitted

Customer Letters and Labels

Occasionally, you may have a need to send standard information to a customer, such as change of address, or to chase up an overdue payment. All of the necessary information needed for these letters is taken from your records.

A number of the more common standard letters are provided with Sage 50, but alternatively there is also the option to create new ones. These new letters can then be stored for future use.

1 From the Customers window, select the customer or customers you want to send a letter to

2 Click the Letters button on the Customers toolbar to bring up the Customer Letters list

3 Click on Letters then select the required letter

4 Click Preview to view the letter and enter Criteria

5 If correct, click Print, then OK

6 Click here to close

Don't forget

Remember to select a customer from the list before clicking the Letters button.

31

Hot tip

To send the same letter (e.g. change of address) to all your customers, first deselect any customers using the Clear button, then select them all using the Swap button on the Customers toolbar before carrying out Steps 2-6.

The Customer Statement

To keep customers up-to-date about their financial position, customer statements should be sent out on a regular basis, normally once a month. The statement shows details of all recorded customer transactions, together with a balance figure.

1 From the Customers window, first select the customers you want statements for, then click on the Statements button to bring up the Customer Statements window

2 Click on Layouts and choose the statement you require

3 Click the Preview button

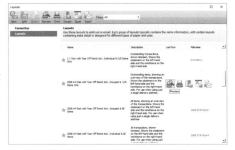

4 Wait for the report to generate and the Criteria box to appear

5 Enter Transaction Date from and to

6 Choose whether to Exclude Later Payments

7 Click OK to preview the statement

8 Use the Zoom button on the preview to zoom in or out if you need to check any statement detail

9 Click Print to print the statement, then Close all windows

3 The Supplier Ledger

See how to create and maintain supplier records within the Supplier (Purchase) Ledger. You will learn how to view details of invoices received and payments made to suppliers using graphs and reports.

The Suppliers Toolbar

The Suppliers toolbar has many similar buttons to the Customers toolbar, and again provides you with facilities for setting up records, checking supplier activity, recording invoices, credit notes and reporting.

 New   Creates a new Supplier Record

 Edit   Opens a Supplier Record

 Price lists   To set up a Supplier Price List

 Activity   View Supplier Activity

 Aged balances   View Supplier Aged Balances

 Batch invoice   Record Supplier Invoices

 Batch credit   Record Supplier Credit Notes

 Disputes   Opens the Disputed Items window

 Labels   To Print Supplier Labels

 Letters   To Print Standard Letters to Suppliers

 Reports   To Run Supplier Reports

Creating Supplier Records

Within this window you can view, edit or delete a supplier record. If a supplier is also a customer you can automatically offset values from supplier and customer invoices against one another. With all of the details to hand, to add a new supplier do the following:

1 Select Suppliers from the Sage 50 navigation bar

2 Click on the New button on the Suppliers toolbar to bring up a blank Supplier Record

3 Use Details to store basic supplier information

4 Use the O/B button if an Opening Balance is required

Hot tip

Until you are familiar with Sage 50, use the New wizard for simple step-by-step instructions for entering a new supplier record.

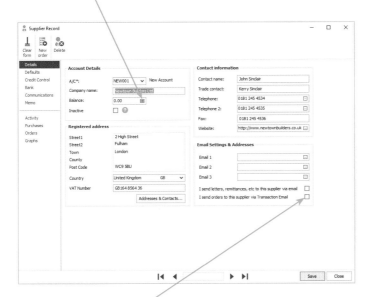

5 Tick here if orders are sent electronically

6 Enter credit terms using the Credit Control option and the Bank to record bank details for payment transfers

7 Click Save to store the Supplier Record

8 Enter a new record or click Close to finish

Don't forget

Always start with the Account Code when entering a new record.

Using Filter

The Filter function available within the Suppliers window can help save you valuable time when searching for specific information regarding supplier transactions. The following example shows you how to produce a list of suppliers you owe money to:

Filter is new in the latest versions of Sage 50 Accounts and is also available within other program windows, such as Customers, Products, Departments and Invoicing. It was formerly called the Search feature.

1 Click on Filter in the Suppliers window to bring up the Filter window

Filter

2 Select Where in the first column

3 Select Balance in this field

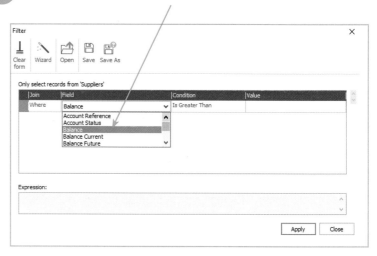

4 Select Is Greater Than in the Condition column

5 Enter zero in the Value field

6 Click Apply and Close to return to the Suppliers window

7 Note that only records matching the filter are displayed. The title bar indicates the filter is applied

8 To cancel the filter and show all records, click this icon

Hot tip

To filter using part information, select the Is Equal To condition and precede the Value with the symbol $. For example, use $W1 and the field Account Address Line 5 to filter for all suppliers in the London W1 area.

36

Supplier Activity

This feature enables you to view each supplier's transactions in detail. If less complete information is required, you can define a transaction or date range to limit the view:

1 From the Suppliers window, select the supplier you want to look at, then click on Activity

2 Select a transaction – all items appear in the lower pane

3 Use the scroll bar to move through all the transactions

4 Click here to select another range of transactions

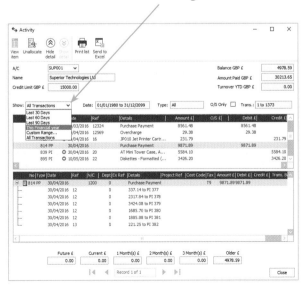

5 Click Close to return to the Suppliers window

Hot tip

To bring up the relevant Product Purchase Order just click on the Edit button on any Purchase Invoice (PI) transaction.

Don't forget

Note that the following codes indicate the transaction type:

PI = Purchase Invoice
PP = Purchase Payment
PR = Purchase Receipt
PC = Purchase Credit Note
PD = Discount on a Purchase Payment
PA = Purchase Payment on Account

Supplier Aged Balance

Aged balance is the term given to the time lapse of outstanding debt, whether owed to you or by you. Sage 50 lets you view the amount of money you owe your suppliers, grouped on the age of the debt. It is common practice for businesses to give 30 days credit, but other terms are sometimes negotiated. Sage 50 default aged periods are 30, 60 and 90 days.

Don't forget

The age period is set through Supplier Defaults from the Settings menu. You can base it on either calendar months or a period of days, specified by you. Remember also that ageing is relative to the program date.

1 From the Suppliers window, click on the supplier you require (or ensure none are selected to view all) and select the Aged balances button from the toolbar to open the Aged Balances window

2 Enter the date to be used for the Aged Balances report

3 Enter the Include Payments Up To date

4 For a transaction breakdown, select a supplier and click the Detailed view button on the toolbar

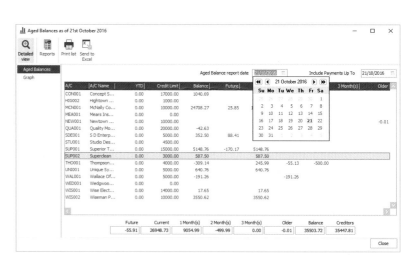

Hot tip

If you need to enter a date only a few days either side of that displayed, simply use the cursor up or down keys on the keyboard.

5 To see a graph format, select Graph on the navigation bar or to export the details to an Excel spreadsheet, simply click the Send to Excel button on the toolbar

6 Click Close to return to the Sage Desktop

Recording Supplier Invoices

Invoices received from your suppliers can be entered a few at a time using the Batch Supplier Invoice window. You have full flexibility using this option, such as posting each invoice item to a different nominal account if need be, or allocating to a different VAT code, such as from default VAT to zero VAT. To enter invoices, do the following:

1 From the Suppliers toolbar, click Batch invoice to bring up the Batch Supplier Invoice window

2 Click here and select the supplier Account Code

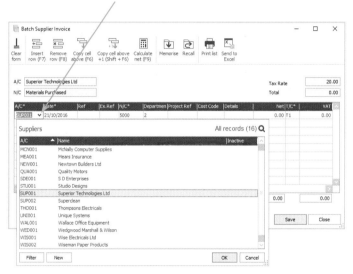

3 Enter the Date and other invoice details, amending the Nominal (N/C) and Tax (T/C) codes if necessary

4 Enter the invoice number in the Ref field

5 Add additional supplier invoices as required

6 When finished, click Save and Yes to update the nominal ledger and supplier details (details posted), then Close

7 Note that the Supplier record now displays a new balance

Beware

Always check that the correct tax code has been selected for the VAT to avoid errors later. Sage 50 enters T1 (standard rate) for you by default. You may need to change this to T0 for transactions which are zero rated or to T9 for any not involving VAT.

Don't forget

Remember that with batch invoices, no printouts are generated of the transaction entered. Use activity reports if you require a paper copy.

Don't forget

'Posting' means updating the Nominal Ledger and relevant supplier's details. If you do not wish to save this batch, choose the Clear form button and start again.

Supplier Credit Notes

Occasionally, goods ordered from suppliers may arrive damaged or incomplete. The supplier issues you a credit note reducing the amount owed. Credit notes are recorded using the Batch credit option from the Suppliers window.

If a credit note contains a number of items, for your benefit it is advisable to enter each transaction individually, but giving them the same account code, date and reference. Sage 50 groups these together and lists them as a single credit note. You can then view the note in more detail using Activity from the Suppliers window.

Hot tip

To reveal if there is more detail available for an entry, just double-click on that entry line.

Don't forget

It is always advisable to check the changes you have made by noting the before and after outstanding balance. This will save time later if a mistake has been made.

Hot tip

Enter the invoice number that the credit note refers to in the Reference (Ex.Ref) box for identification. This will then appear in the Transactions details.

1 From the Suppliers window click the Batch credit button

2 Enter supplier Account Code or use the Finder button

3 The screen displays the defaults for the nominal account code posting, VAT rate to be applied and department

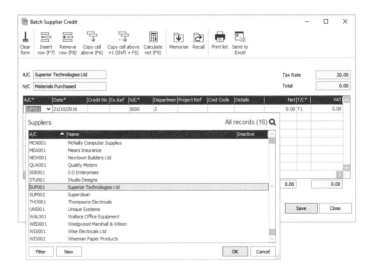

4 Enter credit details for each supplier as per batch invoice

5 Check all values are correct and click Save then Yes to post the details, No to start again or Cancel to return

6 Click Close to return to the Suppliers window

Supplier Letters and Labels

As with Customers, Sage 50 includes the facility to produce preformatted letters and labels for your suppliers. You can also create whatever standard letters or label layouts you wish. All the necessary address information is taken from stored supplier details.

For example, to produce the standard letter informing suppliers of your change of address, do the following:

Hot tip

The Credit Control window has an option to Restrict mailing. Use this to control who you send mailshots to.

1 From the Suppliers window, select the suppliers you want to send the letter to

2 Click the Letters button on the Suppliers toolbar to bring up the Supplier Letters list

3 Click on Letters, select the required letter and click Preview

4 If correct, click Print, then OK

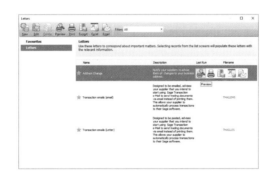

5 When done, click Close

Beware

Always remember to check that the correct paper, labels and printer type have been selected before printing to avoid wasting time and paper.

Labels

To produce address labels for your suppliers, click the Labels button from the Suppliers window then carry out Steps 2-5 as above.

Supplier Reports

You can generate a wide range of detailed reports on your suppliers. These reports are produced from the information you entered about suppliers and their transactions. Sage 50 already has a considerable number of reports set up, but if any further reports are required you can create them using the Report Designer (see Chapter 12). To run or view a supplier report:

1 Click on the Reports button in the Suppliers toolbar

2 Click here on the required group and select a report

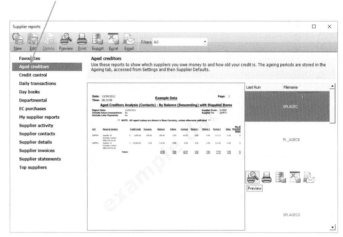

3 Click on the Preview button to begin producing the report

4 If a Criteria box appears, enter the from and to details

5 Tick the Transactions or Payments options as required, then click OK

6 After printing, close all windows

4 The Nominal Ledger

This chapter explains the important role played by the Nominal Ledger and how its contents detail the flow of money in and out of the business. You will be shown how to analyse these account transactions using graphs and activity reports.

The Nominal Toolbar

The Nominal toolbar buttons provide you with facilities for setting up records, viewing account activity, making journal entries, setting up prepayments and accruals, working on the Chart of Accounts and reporting.

New — Creates a new Nominal Account

Edit — Opens a Nominal Record

Activity — View a Nominal Account's Activity

Journal entry — Enter Journal double-entries

Journal reversal — Process Nominal Ledger Reversals

Prepayments — Enter Nominal Ledger Prepayments

Accruals — Enter Nominal Ledger Accruals

Chart of accounts — Opens the Chart of Accounts

Reports — To Run Nominal Ledger Report

The Nominal Ledger

The Nominal Ledger, also referred to as the General Ledger, is a grouped analysis of your sales and purchase transactions. For example, when a sales or purchase invoice is posted to the sales or purchase ledger, Sage 50 records it in the Nominal Ledger against the appropriate Nominal account number.

It therefore contains all the accounts for your business, e.g. sales, purchases, expenses, VAT, cash and bank, sundry income, fixed assets, liabilities, capital and owner's drawings, etc. However, it does not keep details of debtors and creditors. These are held in the respective sales and purchase ledgers.

The Nominal accounts let you see where your money is or has gone. Information from here is used in the production of management reports to tell you how your business is performing.

1 Select Nominal codes from the Sage 50 navigation bar

2 Click here to drill down further in a Nominal Area

To help you work with the Nominal Ledger, here are some of the standard nominal accounts used by Sage 50:

- Asset Accounts from 0001 to 1999
- Liability Accounts from 2000 to 3999
- Income Accounts from 4000 to 4999
- Purchase Accounts from 5000 to 5999
- Direct Expenses from 6000 to 6999
- Overheads from 7000 to 9999

45

To see a list of all nominal codes, simply select the List view option instead of the Analyser view.

In Sage 50, you can choose a standard set of nominal accounts during installation, unless in the Startup Wizard you decided to create your own nominal structure. Note that the latter option only creates the Control Accounts for you.

Nominal Records

You can tailor the nominal accounts to exactly meet your needs by using the Nominal Record window. You have the facility to add, edit and delete nominal accounts as well as viewing transactions posted to each account on a monthly basis.

Using the Record window you can also set budget values for each month of your financial year for a particular nominal account. You can also compare the actual monthly figures against the budget values to keep track of how close you are to meeting targets. To add a nominal account record and set budgets:

Hot tip

Keep track of your business performance by initially entering monthly budget and prior year values, then regularly compare these against the actual values.

1 Click the New button from the Nominal codes toolbar to bring up a blank Nominal Record

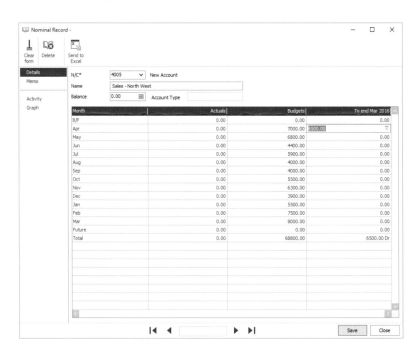

Beware

You cannot delete a Nominal Code whilst there is still a balance on it.

2 In the N/C field, enter a new nominal account code

3 Press the Tab key and note that this is a New Account

4 Enter the new account Name, Budget and Prior Year values

5 Click Save to store details or Clear form to start again

Viewing Nominal Transactions

You can view your Nominal Ledger transactions by using:

- **Graphs**

- **Activity reports**

- **List/Table formats**

Transaction Analysis using Graphs

Sage 50 allows you to displays your nominal codes in the form of pie charts. From the main pie chart you can then choose individual areas and drill down further for more detail.

1 From the Nominal codes window, select the Graph view option to display the Nominal Ledger pie chart

The Graph view has been updated in the latest versions of Sage 50, with all information now displayed in easy to interpret 3D pie charts.

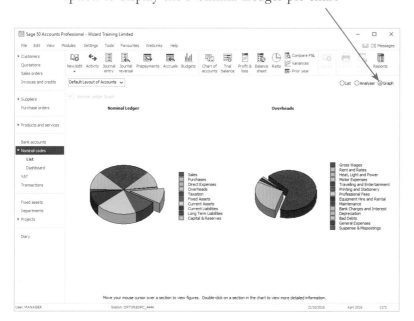

To include Sage 50 graphs in other documents, simply press Print Screen on your keyboard and then use Paste followed by Crop to insert it into another document or chart.

2 To view more information in the chart, hover your cursor over areas on the chart

3 Double-click a section of the chart to display a pie chart for that section. You can then drill down further

4 Click on a colour in the key list to highlight a slice

...cont'd

Viewing Nominal Account Activity

You will occasionally need to view transactions that have been posted to the nominal ledger accounts. To do this from the Nominal codes window, select List view then do the following:

1 Click on the nominal account you wish to view

2 Click on the toolbar Activity button to bring up the Activity window

3 Select a transaction – all items appear in the lower pane

4 Use the scroll bar to move through all the transactions

5 Click on Show to select another range of transactions

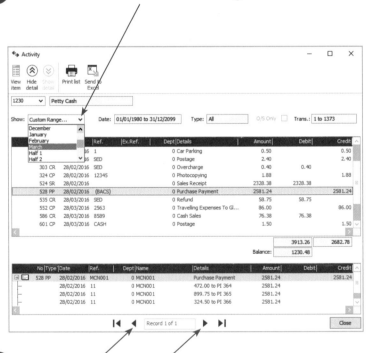

6 Use the previous and next buttons to view other nominal accounts, if more than one is selected in Step 1

7 Close the window to return to the Nominal codes screen

Transaction Codes

Transactions in the Activity window are indicated by a type (Tp) or transaction code, allocated by Sage 50 as follows:

BR (Bank Receipt)	SD (Discount on Sales Receipt)
BP (Bank Payment)	SA (Sales Receipt on Account)
CP (Cash Payment)	PI (Purchase Invoice)
CR (Cash Receipt)	PP (Purchase Payment)
JD (Journal Debit)	PR (Purchase Receipt)
JC (Journal Credit)	PC (Purchase Credit)
SI (Sales Invoice)	PD (Discount on Purchase Payment)
SR (Sales Receipt)	PA (Purchase Payment on Account)
SP (Sales Payment	VP (Visa Credit Payments)
SC (Sales Credit)	VR (Visa Credit Receipts)

Using Filter

It is sometimes handy to reduce the number of records displayed in the Nominal codes window or on your reports to only those that match specific criteria. This will save you having to look through many records for the information needed. For example, to list only control accounts in the Nominal codes window:

1 Click Filter in the Nominal codes window `Filter`

2 Select Where, choose Account Type Code and Is Equal To then select Control Account from the drop-down list

3 Click on the Apply button, then click Close to finish

You can tell at a glance if a filter is being applied to a list because it will not display the words 'All Records' next to the Filter button.

The Number (No.) column shows the transaction number in the Audit Trail. You will need this number if you wish to amend or delete a transaction using the File, Maintenance, Corrections option.

A Filter remains applied to a list until you click the Remove Filter icon.

49

Don't forget

The rules for debits and credits are as follows: Debit the account which receives the value; Credit the account which gives the value.

Don't forget

If you post a journal entry incorrectly, Sage 50 lets you use the Reversal button from the Journals toolbar to remove the entry. You can then simply re-enter the journal correctly. Just click on the Journal Reversal button and follow the prompts to print the Nominal Ledger Day Book and back up your data before you process the reversal.

Journal
reversal

The Journal

The Journal allows you to make transfers between any of your nominal account codes regardless of type (Asset, Liability, Income or Expenditure), provided you adhere to double-entry bookkeeping principles. It lets you enter transactions which may not be covered within the standard Sage 50 facilities.

It is a useful source of reference for these non-regular transactions and can reduce errors by providing a list (audit trail) for checking purposes. Examples of these transactions include correction of errors and transfer of monies, as well as the purchase and sale of fixed assets on credit.

As stated, the Journal follows double-entry bookkeeping principles, i.e. the value of the credit transaction must equal the value of the debit transaction. Each line of the Journal Entry table represents a single transaction; therefore, there must be at least two transactions in the journal (a credit and a debit).

However, this does not mean that you must post a single credit item for every single debit item. You can, for example, post several debits but only one balancing credit, and vice versa. Provided the net difference between your postings is always zero (i.e. the total value of credits equals the total value of debits), you can then post the Journal.

'Skeleton' Journals

For journals that you make regularly, payments from a bank to a credit card account for example, Sage 50 lets you save the details of that journal entry so that you can use it the next time without having to enter it all again. This is called a 'skeleton'. Some skeleton journals were set up at installation, such as the VAT Liability Transfer Journal.

To save a skeleton journal, click on the Memorise button after you have set up the journal. To load a skeleton journal, click on the Recall button, select the journal you need and click on the Load button. You can even load one of the skeleton journals provided by Sage 50, modify it to suit your needs, then save it.

Reversals

In Sage 50 you can reverse an incorrectly posted journal entry using the Journal Reversal option from the Nominal codes window. Use F1 Help for a full explanation of reversing a journal.

Making a Journal Entry

Here is an example of how you would make a journal entry for capital introduced into the business for use in the bank current (1200) and petty cash (1230) accounts:

1 From the Nominal codes toolbar, click Journal entry

2 Use the Calendar button if a different date is required

3 Enter a Reference and details for both the credit and debit transactions. Ex.Ref is optional

4 Note, the default Tax code of T9 is entered for you

5 Check total Debit and Credit are equal and a zero balance is displayed in the Balance box

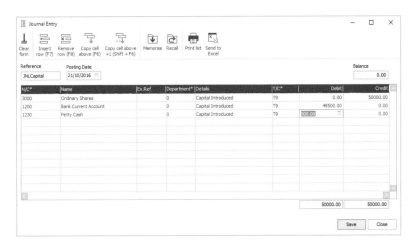

6 To process your journal, click Save or Clear form to cancel

7 Click Close to return to the Nominal codes window

Note that Sage 50 will not automatically calculate VAT, or post it to the VAT Control Account. If VAT is required, enter each VAT element as a separate line, with a debit or credit to the appropriate VAT Control Account.

51

Beware

When you make a manual journal entry, VAT is neither calculated for you nor posted to the VAT Control Account.

Hot tip

If you use a journal entry regularly, save it as a skeleton using the Memorise button, so you can recreate it quickly and easily later.

Memorise

Beware

Before saving the journal, always ensure the Balance box shows zero. If the value of the credit transactions does not equal the value of the debit transactions, then Sage 50 issues a warning and will not let you save the journal.

Setting up Prepayments

To adjust statements and reports for any payments which have to be made in advance, for example rent or insurance, there is a Prepayments option available from the Nominal codes window. This allows for a payment to be shown as spread over the number of months it refers to, not just the month it was paid in.

After setting up a prepayment, when you run the Month End procedure the correct monthly figure is posted to the appropriate account. All you have to do is to remember to post a suitable payment for the full amount from the bank to the appropriate nominal account.

1 From the Nominal codes toolbar, click Prepayments to bring up the Prepayments window

Hot tip

Just click on the Wizard button to let the Prepayments Wizard guide you through setting up a prepayment:

Wizard

2 Enter the relevant nominal account code (N/C)

3 Enter Details, Net Value of prepayment and the number of Months prepayment covers (maximum of 12)

Hot tip

Use F6 key to save time and reduce errors when copying data from a previous entry.

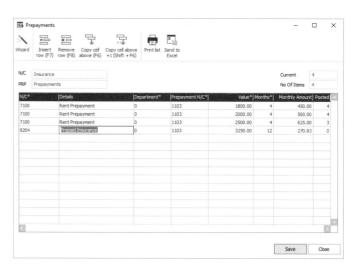

4 Note that the monthly rate is entered for you

Don't forget

No accounting takes place when prepayment details are saved. Journal Entry postings are only made when the Month End, Post Prepayments option is run.

5 Click Save to accept the prepayment details

6 Click Close to return to the Nominal codes window

52

Setting up Accruals

The Accruals option allows the accounts to be adjusted for any payments you make in one accounting period, which in fact relate to a previous period, such as a gas or electricity bill.

In this example, the transaction would be entered using the Accrual and Gas or Electricity accounts. When the charges actually fall due and the bill is paid, the payment transaction is applied to the Accrual account, not the Gas or Electricity account.

As with the prepayments option, the accruals are posted as part of your month end procedure using the Period End, Month End option. This procedure automatically updates the audit trail and nominal accounts records.

1 From the Nominal codes window, click Accruals

2 Enter Nominal account code, or use the Finder button

3 Enter Details, the estimated total Net Value of accrual and number of Months for the accrual

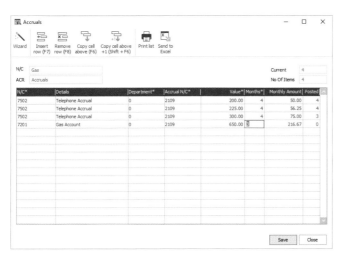

4 Monthly accrual is calculated for you

5 Click Save to accept accrual details

6 Click Close to return to the Nominal codes window

The Posted column shows how many postings have been made using the Month End Post prepayment option.

No accounting takes place when accrual details are saved. Journal Entry postings are only made when the Month End, Post Accruals option is run.

If you have already set up some accrual entries, these appear in the Accruals window when it opens. Just add your new Accrual at the end of the list.

The Chart of Accounts

During installation, Sage 50 created a simple Chart of Accounts suitable for standard reporting, such as Profit and Loss, Balance Sheet, Budget and Prior Year Reports.

It may be that the default account names are not suitable for your business, so the Chart of Accounts can be customised to meet your business requirements. New category types can be introduced into the accounts or current categories edited to reflect, for example, the actual items sold within your business.

The Chart of Accounts is subdivided into the following default report category types:

Profit & Loss
- Sales
- Purchases
- Direct Expenses
- Overheads
- Taxation

Balance Sheet
- Fixed Assets
- Current Assets
- Current Liabilities
- Long Term Liabilities
- Capital & Reserves

54

1 To examine the Chart of Accounts' facilities, click the Chart of accounts button from the Nominal codes window

2 If you want to look at a chart, select it from the list and click Edit

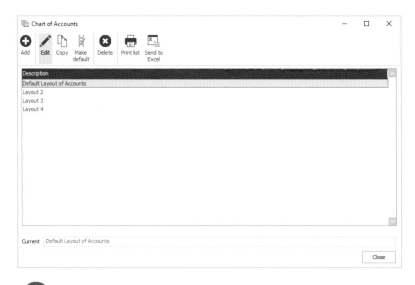

3 To create a new Chart of Accounts, click the Add button

4 To use a particular Chart of Accounts, simply highlight it from the list and click the Make default button

Always check that the name of the layout you selected appears automatically in the 'Current' text box.

5 When finished, click Close to return to the Nominal codes window

Creating a Chart of Accounts Layout
Do the following to add a new Chart of Accounts layout:

1 Click Chart of accounts from the Nominal codes window

2 Click Add in the Chart of Accounts window

3 Enter the name of your new Chart of Accounts layout

4 Click Add to continue

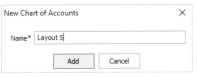

5 Click on a category and change its description to that required in your financial reports

6 Enter (or amend) the headings for each range of nominal accounts in the selected category and set the range of nominal accounts to be included for each selected category in the Low and High boxes

7 Click Check to see if you've made any errors then click Save, or Close to discard

8 To print your Chart of Accounts, click Printer, or click Preview to just view on your screen, then click Run

Don't forget

If you elected to create your own Chart of Accounts during the Startup Wizard, the default Chart of Accounts will not contain any category accounts.

Hot tip

Use the Check button to quickly find any nominal account errors in your new layout.

Nominal Reports

To print or preview reports using the nominal data already entered into the system, use the Reports option from the Nominal codes window. Sage 50 already supplies a considerable number of pre-installed reports to suit most needs, but you can create additional custom reports using the Sage Report Designer. See Chapter 12 for more details on creating reports.

To print a Nominal Ledger report, do the following:

1 From the Nominal codes toolbar, click Reports

2 Click on the report group and select the report required

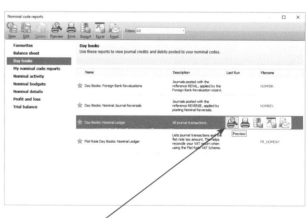

3 Click the Preview button to begin generating the report

4 Type the range details or use the Calendar and Finder buttons

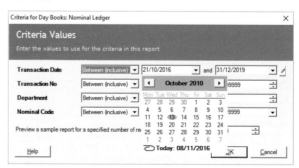

5 Click OK to preview report

Hot tip

You may sometimes find it easier to select nominal accounts from the Nominal codes window instead of entering them in the Criteria box.

5 The Bank

This chapter shows you how to maintain your bank account records and transactions. This includes deposits, payments, transfer of money between bank accounts and adjustments to show bank charges and interest received. It also covers reconciling your statements, processing recurring entries and the production of cheques.

The Bank Toolbar

This toolbar provides features for the recording and maintenance of bank transactions and records. You can perform adjustments, record the transfer of monies, enter receipts, produce statements and reports and even print cheques.

Hot tip

To quickly create a new Bank account, use the New Wizard from the Bank accounts toolbar and work through the simple step-by-step screens.

New/edit	Create New or Edit a Bank Record
Reconcile	Opens Bank Account Reconciliation
Bank payment	Record Bank Payments
Supplier payment	Record Supplier Payments
Remittances	To Print Bank Remittances
Batch	To Record a Batch Purchase Payment
Bank receipt	Record Money Received
Customer receipt	Record Customer Receipts
Bank transfer	Make Bank Transfers
Recurring items	Opens Recurring Entries Window
Cash flow	Opens the Cash Flow Window
Statements	To Print Bank Statements
Cheques	To Print Cheques
Reports	To Run Bank Account Reports

Bank Accounts

There are three main types of bank accounts used in Sage 50:
Bank Accounts, Cash Accounts and Credit Card Accounts.

The Bank account option treats both Bank and Building Societies
as bank accounts. Three bank accounts have already been
automatically set up to include a bank current account, a bank
deposit account and a building society account.

Cash accounts called Petty Cash and Cash Register have also
been set up, but other cash accounts can be added, for example
Emergency Cash or Additional Travel Expenses.

The facility to record your credit card bank details is available and
allows you to monitor any credit card transactions you have made
and keep track of your money. A Company Credit Card account
is provided ready for you to use.

To view the Bank account window:

1 Select Bank accounts from the Sage 50 navigation bar

2 Click on the bank account required, then click on the
appropriate button for the function you wish to carry out

3 When finished, click Close

Sage treats credit
card accounts as bank
accounts. You can also
set up your PayPal and
eBay accounts as bank
accounts.

To have your current
bank balance to hand
when creating new Bank
records.

Depending on the size
of your screen, if all
of the toolbar buttons
will not fit then Sage
50 now groups them
together by activity, such
as Payments, Receipts,
etc. Click on the arrow
head at the base of
the symbol to reveal
additional buttons, as
shown in the Hot Tip on
page 58 opposite.

Bank, Cash & Credit Accounts

As stated, Sage 50 provides three types of bank accounts readily created for you to use:

- **Bank Account** (includes both bank deposit and current account, plus a building society account)

- **Cash Account** (named Petty Cash and Cash Register)

- **Credit Card Account** (company credit card)

These accounts can be edited to match your own details. Accounts can also be added or deleted. To set up your Bank account details:

1 From the Bank accounts window, select account type required and click on the New/edit button in the Bank toolbar

2 Check the details and make changes if necessary

3 Click here to enter Current Balance

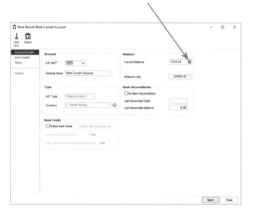

Should the minimum balance fall below the figure entered, it will be displayed in red in the Bank accounts window.

4 Enter Opening Balance and other details then click Save

5 Select Bank Details in the navigation bar and enter any further relevant details

6 Click Save to store details, then Close

Recording Bank Payments

For recording any non-invoiced or one-off payments, use the Payment option from the Bank accounts window. Sage 50 then makes it very easy for you to keep track of where your money goes – simply select the appropriate account, enter the payment and post it.

To record Bank payments:

1 Click on Payments from the Bank toolbar and select Bank payment

2 Use the Finder button to enter Bank account code

3 Enter Date (and transaction Reference if required)

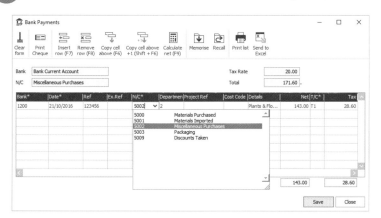

4 Enter a Nominal Code for the payment to be posted to, or use the Finder button as shown

5 Enter Details describing the payment

6 Enter the amount (change Tax Code from default of T1 if necessary)

7 Click Save to post details (update the nominal ledger and the Bank account)

8 Click Close to return to the Bank accounts window

Leave the cheque number blank if you intend on using the Cheques printing option. Cheque numbers will then be automatically generated for you.

Enter a discount value in the discount box, not a percentage, for any invoiced item. The Analysis Total box decreases by the discount value entered.

Use the Remittances button on the Bank accounts toolbar to quickly print a batch of remittances:

Remittances

Supplier Invoice Payments

The Supplier payment option from the Bank accounts toolbar will provide you with a detailed transaction list of any outstanding invoice items, credit notes and payments made on account to suppliers. To record payment of a supplier invoice do the following:

1 In the Bank accounts window, select the account required (e.g. Bank Current Account) and click Payments, then select Supplier Payment from the drop-down list

2 Enter Supplier account code in the Payee field

3 Use the Calendar button if payment date is different

4 Enter cheque number if required (see the *Don't forget* tip in the margin)

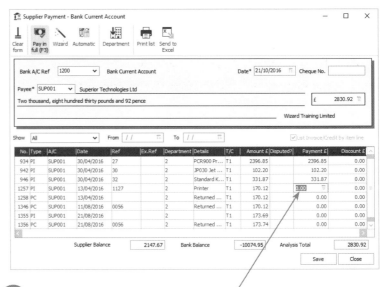

5 Enter value in the Payment box for part-payment or click on the Pay in full (F3) button to enter full amount

6 Repeat Step 5 for any remaining transactions

7 Click Save to save payment details, then Close to return to the Bank accounts window

Batch Purchase Payments

You can list all outstanding purchase invoices, purchase credit notes and purchase payments on account for all suppliers, using the Batch supplier payment option from the Bank accounts window. The transactions are sorted in order, firstly by supplier and then by transaction number.

Outstanding transactions can be paid in three ways:

● All transactions paid in full

● Individual transactions paid in full

● Individual transactions paid in part

To record full or part payments:

1 Select account required and click Payments, then select Batch Supplier Payments from the drop-down list

2 To pay ALL outstanding transactions click Pay All

3 To make INDIVIDUAL full payments, select a transaction and click on the Pay in Full button

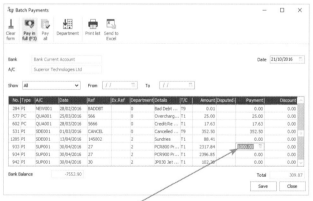

4 For a PART PAYMENT simply enter the amount in the Payment box

5 When finished, click Save, or Clear form to start again

6 Click Close

Hot tip

You can pay a transaction either in full or part.

Don't forget

All outstanding transactions can be paid in full in one go using the Pay all button, but note that there will only be one posting.

Don't forget

If any of the selected transactions are in dispute, Sage 50 displays a warning message.

Bank Receipts

To record any non-invoiced or miscellaneous payments you receive, the Bank receipt option from the Bank accounts window is used. These items are allocated a specific nominal code for analysis purposes so a check can be made on monies received.

To enter receipt of money:

1 From the Bank account window click on Bank receipt

2 In Bank Receipts select the appropriate Bank account

3 Ensure the required Date is entered

4 Enter a suitable Reference, such as a cheque number

5 Select a Nominal Account Code to post the receipt to and give Details

6 Enter the Net value

7 Repeat Steps 2-6 to record further receipts, then click Save to post transactions

8 When finished, close all windows

Recording Customer Receipts

The Customer option from the Bank accounts window is used to record money received from your customers. When the customer's account reference is entered, any outstanding invoices appear automatically in the Customer Receipt window.

To record full or part payments:

1 From the Bank accounts window, select the bank account required and click on the Customer receipt button

2 Enter a customer Account Code to display all items not fully paid for that customer

3 Check Date and enter a paying in Reference, if possible

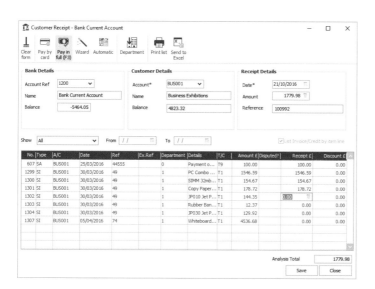

4 If FULL payment has been received, select a transaction and click Pay in full (F3)

5 If this is a PART payment enter the amount received

6 Enter any further receipts then click Save to process them

7 When finished, close all windows

You can pay an invoice in full or part but you cannot allocate an amount more than the item value.

Use the Customer Receipt button to record full and part-payments, payments on account against your sales invoices and to allocate credit notes.

Sage 50 automatically warns you of any disputed items.

Bank Transfers

Sometimes you will need to transfer money from one bank account to another. You can record this using the Bank transfer option from the Bank Accounts window or by making a journal entry.

To make a bank transfer, do the following:

Don't forget

You can also record a Bank Transfer through a journal entry.

1 From the Bank accounts window, select the bank you wish to move the money from

2 Click Bank transfer to open the Bank Transfer window

3 Enter the Nominal Code of the bank account you are transferring to

4 Enter a Reference and appropriate Details

5 Check the Date is correct and enter the transfer amount

Don't forget

Sage 50 enters today's date in the Date box for you, but this can be altered if necessary.

6 Click Save to process or Clear form to start again

7 Click Close to finish

Recurring Entries

For payments which remain consistent and are paid on a monthly basis, for example rent and electricity, the Recurring items option can be used from the Bank accounts window. This feature is also useful for standing orders and direct debits and prevents payments such as these from being overlooked. Each month, these transactions need posting to update your bank accounts and ledgers.

If there are any outstanding recurring entries, Sage 50 reminds you on startup and asks if you wish to post them. To add a recurring entry:

1 Select Recurring items from the Bank accounts window then click the Add button

2 Select the transaction type from the drop-down list

3 Enter the Bank Account Code

4 Enter a Nominal Code to post the transaction to

5 Give Reference and Details, then enter Posting Frequency data

6 Enter Net amount and check the Tax Code

7 Click OK to return to the Recurring Items window

8 Click Process and Process All to process the recurring entries, then click Close to finish

Beware

Note that recurring entries need processing each month before you can run the Month or Year End procedures.

Don't forget

Sage 50 will only let you post journal credits when you post journal debits of the same value, and vice versa.

Don't forget

The Last Posted box always remains blank until the new entry is saved and processed.

Hot tip

If you need to stop a monthly payment, simply click the Suspend Posting box. This is handy for those payments which do not need posting every month.

Add / Edit Recurring Entry

Recurring Entry From / To

Bank A/C*	1200	Bank Current Account
Nominal Code*	0030	Office Equipment

Recurring Entry Details

Transaction Type	Bank/Cash/Credit Card Payment
Transaction Ref	DD/STO
Transaction Details	Office Furniture Lease
Department*	0 Default

Posting Frequency

Every*	1 Month(s)	Total Required Postings	24
Start Date*	21/10/2016	Finish Date	21/09/2018
Next Posting Date	21/10/2016	Suspend Posting ?	☐
Last Posted			

Posting Amounts

Net Amount	70.00	Tax Code*	T1 20.00	VAT 14.00

OK   Cancel

Generating Cheques

This feature provides you with the ability to print cheques automatically for a particular bank account. All Purchase Payments (type PP) and Purchase Payments on Account (type PA) transactions not previously printed and with blank references, are listed in the Print Cheques window. This is how to print cheques using the cheque generator:

Beware

If no transactions are selected, the program will print cheques for ALL the transactions.

1 From the Bank accounts window, select the required bank account and click on the Cheques button

2 Allocate a new Cheque Number if required

3 Select the transactions requiring cheques

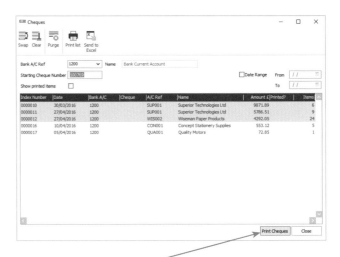

Hot tip

You can now print a cheque for a supplier without first having to set up an account.

4 Click Print Cheques

5 Select the layout required, then click Run

6 Click Yes if cheques have been printed correctly, then Close

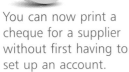

68

The Bank Statement

Sage 50 provides you with the facility to print your bank statements out at any time, showing all reconciled bank payments and receipts. These statements show the transactions made to and from each bank account, and prove useful for cross-referencing purposes when checking for any transaction omissions or additions. To print a report in bank statement format:

1 From the Bank accounts window select the desired account and click on Statements

2 Select Preview from output options and click Run

3 Enter Transaction Date range here and click OK to preview

4 Click Print, then OK from the print dialog box

5 Click here when finished

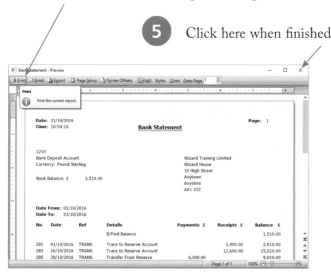

Hot tip

To use this facility effectively, make sure that you enter all Bank transactions accurately and completely so that the Sage 50 Bank statements match your actual bank statements.

Hot tip

You can also save the Bank Statement reports as a file for use at a later date. Simply click on the Save As button in the Report Preview window.

Don't forget

To bring up previously-saved statements, click Open and select the required statement from the list.

Bank Account Reconciliation

Bank reconciliation is the process of matching up your computer bank records and transactions with those shown on the statements received from your bank.

The Reconcile window displays transactions which have not been previously reconciled. After entering the date of the statement, you can work through your bank statement, matching the transactions recorded in Sage 50. If necessary, you should make any adjustments needed to ensure that Sage 50 bank accounts accurately reflect the actual transactions processed by your bank. To reconcile a bank account:

Don't forget

Before you select any transactions to reconcile, always check that the opening balance shown in the Bank Reconciliation window is the same as the opening balance on your actual bank statement.

Beware

A bank account cannot be reconciled if the check box No Bank Reconciliation is ticked on the bank record.

1 From the Bank accounts window select the bank account to be reconciled, then click the Reconcile button

2 Enter the closing balance of your bank statement

3 Enter the date of the bank statement, complete details, then click OK

4 Click each transaction that matches the bank statement

5 Click Match to add transactions to the lower pane

6 When finished, click Reconcile

7 Where the Difference between the balances is not zero, add the required adjustment value (see page 71)

...cont'd

Bank reconciliation will only work correctly provided that a number of important rules are followed:

● The opening balance shown in the Reconcile window must match the opening balance on your actual bank statement.

If for some reason they are different, you will need to check why and make the necessary adjustments. One way of doing this is to view the selected bank's activity from within the nominal ledger. To see if a transaction is reconciled, check the Bank column in the Audit Trail, where: R = reconciled and N = not reconciled.

● Work through your actual bank statement progressively one line at a time, clicking on the corresponding transaction entry in the Reconcile window to highlight it.

● If you come across a transaction on your bank statement not shown in Sage 50, you should record this transaction immediately using the Adjustments facility.

● Check everything carefully. When you are satisfied that all transactions for reconciliation have been selected and any adjustments made, the Difference box should show zero.

Making Adjustments

1 From the Reconcile window, click the Adjust... button, select the Adjustment Type, then click OK

Adjust...

2 Enter the Nominal Code of the account to receive the adjustment

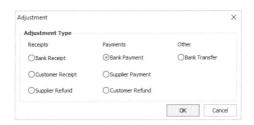

3 Enter the adjustment details and value

4 If correct, click Save, then Close

Don't forget

Thoroughly check all transactions on the bank statement against the Reconcile list. Also check that the reconcile balance box matches the closing statement balance.

Hot tip

As you select and match each transaction, note that the Balance and Difference values automatically change.

Hot tip

Use the Adjust... button or Bank payments, receipts and transfers facilities to record any additional transactions shown on your bank statement, e.g. charges, cashpoint withdrawals, etc.

Bank Reports

There is a wide range of ready-to-use bank reports provided by Sage 50. These reports outline your bank details and transactions and help you keep track of your bank finances. It is advisable that you regularly print out the standard reports, such as Day Books, once you have entered the relevant transactions.

1 From the Bank accounts window, click the Reports button to bring up the Bank reports window

2 Click on a report group and select the report required

3 Click the Preview button

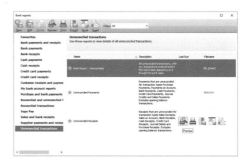

4 Enter any Criteria if required, click OK then Print

Cash Flow Window

A useful feature in Sage 50 is the cash flow display, showing outstanding payments, receipts and recurring entries.

1 From the toolbar, click the Cash flow button

2 Click Print if required

3 Use Send to Excel to export the details

4 When done, click Close

Hot tip

When you have become familiar with the various reports, you can save time by sending them straight to the printer without the need to preview. Simply select Print instead of Preview in Step 3.

Hot tip

You can save a report as a file in a number of useful formats, such as Microsoft Excel, Text file or Comma Separated Value (CSV).

Hot tip

If you choose to print the report, the Windows Print dialog box appears. Use this to select which pages to print and change your printer settings if necessary.

6 Products

Learn how to create and maintain records for the products you buy and sell, and how to set up product codes. You will also see how to monitor stock levels, record movement of stock and how to analyse various product transactions.

The Products Toolbar

The Products and services toolbar provides features for the recording and maintenance of product records and transactions. You have the facility to record the movement of your products and make any adjustments and/or transfer of stock. Product activity can be analysed and reports generated.

Hot tip

To quickly create a new Product record, use the New Wizard from the Products and services toolbar and work through the simple step-by-step screens.

Wizard

Edit	Opens a Product Record
Price lists	To Set up a Price List
Activity	View a Product Activity
Shortfall	To Run the Product Shortfall Generator
Adjustment in	Make Stock In Adjustments
Adjustment out	Make Stock Out Adjustments
Stock transfer	Record Stock Transfers
Stock take	Automatically Make Stock Adjustments
Check bill of materials	Check Make-Up Capability For Stock
Returns	For Recording Stock Returns
Allocations	For Recording Stock Allocations
Labels	To Produce Product Labels
Reports	To Run Product Reports

The Product Record

Sage 50 allows you to create, edit or delete records for all the products your business sells. Once these records have been set up, all you need to do is enter a product code and the details will be automatically included for you on any product invoice, credit note or order you create.

From the Product Record window you can view the sales price and quantity in stock for each product. Use the Products option to:

- Create and maintain records for all products bought or sold

- Record product movements

- Analyse product transactions using tables or graphs

- Set up a Bill of Materials

- Keep track of your stock levels

From the Product Record window, as well as being able to view the Sales Price and Quantity in Stock, you can view the Product Code and Description for each product.

1 Click Products and services from the navigation bar

2 To view Product details, select a product and click on the Edit button

3 Click Save if any changes have been made, else Close

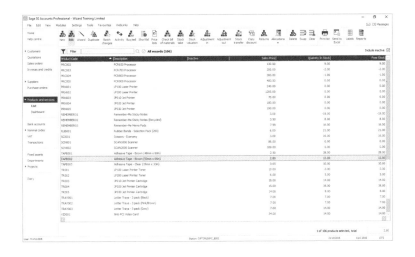

Opening Balances need setting up for your products. Follow the same procedures as for your customers, suppliers, nominal and bank accounts.

Once a product record has been set up, take care before deleting it, even if there is zero stock and no more is expected. It may still belong to a part allocated order.

Use the Stock take option to make adjustments to your stock levels after you have completed a stock take. All you need to do is enter the current stock levels for your products and Sage 50 makes all of the necessary adjustments for you.

...cont'd

Entering a new Product Record

1 From the Products and services window click on the New button

2 Type a unique Product Code and press Tab

3 Enter Description, check the Nominal sales and VAT code

4 Enter Sales Price here

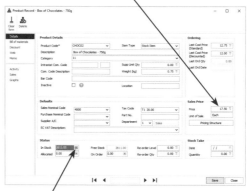

76

5 Click on O/B button then Yes to save changes

6 Check for the correct Date and enter Quantity

7 Enter Cost Price of the Product

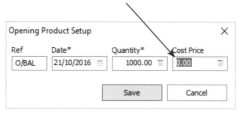

8 Click Save, then Close to return to the Products window

Entering details onto the Product Record

Whilst the Product Record has been designed to accept a considerable amount of detail, not every item is applicable to all products. However, to make reporting more accurate later, you should try to include as much detail as possible about a product when adding records.

Not all of the boxes on the Product Record will accept user entry, though. Sage 50 calculates or generates the following information and enters it for you. It cannot be directly edited.

Allocated   This figure shows the quantity of the product which has been partly or fully allocated on the sales order, but which has not yet been despatched.

Free Stock   Sage 50 calculates the Free Stock as being the In Stock total minus the Allocated stock total.

On Order   Using the Purchase Orders option, this is the quantity of the product which has been put 'on order'.

Last Ord Qty   This shows the amount of stock ordered when the last purchase order for this product was put 'on order'.

Last Ord Date   This shows the date of the last purchase order raised for this product after being put on order.

Cost Price   This is the latest cost price for the product item, entered using the Opening Balance option, the Adjustments In option, Purchase Order Processing or the Global Changes option (useful for updating cost prices for all or selected product items).

When running financial or management reports, you must be aware that Sage 50 will use this latest price even though products already in stock may have actually cost more or less. This must be remembered as this may, on occasion, give distorted figures, such as when calculating the total cost value of a product item in stock.

If stock level falls below the re-order level, the item appears red in the Products window and also appears on the Re-order report.

If you use or propose to use a bar code reader, enter the bar code character string in the product details section of the Product Record.

If you do not enter a Cost Price in the Opening Product Setup box, the product cost is recorded as zero. This could affect some of your financial reports later.

Product Defaults

To save entering repetitive details and to make the process of creating new product records easier, Sage 50 includes the facility to set up various product defaults.

Whenever a new product record is created, certain regular details, e.g. Nominal Code, Tax Code, Department, etc., are asked for. If you use a recording system where these codes remain the same for most of your products, default settings can be set up which will then appear automatically in each new product record without you having to enter them every time. To set up product defaults:

1 From the Sage 50 menu bar, first select Settings, then Product Defaults

2 Enter the Nominal Code to be used by default whenever you create orders and product invoices

3 Select the VAT rate (Tax code) and Purchase nominal code, if relevant

4 Enter Unit of Sale, e.g. 'Each' or 'Box', then choose Category and Department as required

5 Enter the number of decimal places (D.P.) for Quantity and unit sale Price

6 Click OK to save or Cancel to discard any changes

78

Using Filter

Using Filter speeds up the process of searching for specific product records, for example to show products which match a particular description, or those below the re-order stock level. The following example shows how to set up a filter to restrict Product Records to only those with less than 50 in stock:

1 Click on Filter in the Products and services window to bring up the Filter window

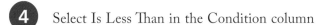

2 Click Where in the first column

3 Select Quantity in stock in this field

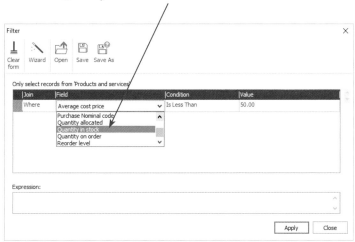

4 Select Is Less Than in the Condition column

5 Enter 50 in the Value field

6 Click Apply and Close to return to the Products window

7 Note that only records matching the search are displayed. The title bar indicates the filter is applied

8 To cancel the filter and show all records, click this icon

Hot tip

The calculator button is a quick and handy way of making an entry in the Value field. It is a small image of a calculator on the right of any monetary field.

Filter is new in the latest versions of Sage 50 Accounts and is also available within other program windows, such as Customers, Products, Departments and Invoicing. It was formerly called the Search feature.

Don't forget

A Filter remains applied to a list until you decide to cancel it.

Bill of Materials

This term relates to a product you hold in stock that is made up from other products you keep. The made-up product is sometimes known as a product assembly and is said to have a Bill of Materials. For example, a first aid kit is a product assembly consisting of various components – bandages, tablets, plasters, etc.

For businesses selling a product made up of other products, it is useful to set up a Bill of Materials. In Sage 50 this feature keeps track of stock levels and can automatically calculate how many products you can make up for sale from the stock you currently hold and at what cost price. To set up a Bill of Materials for a product, do the following:

Use the Transfer button from the Products and services window to increase stock levels of your product assemblies.

1 In the Products and services window, select the product you wish to set up a Bill of Materials for, and click Edit

2 Select Bill of materials from the navigation bar

3 Enter the Product Code for each item

The Bill of Materials table itemises each individual component for the product assembly.

4 Enter the quantity required for product assembly

5 Click Refresh to see how many you can make from stock

6 Click Save to store, or Clear form to start again

7 Click Close

See how many product assemblies you can make up by looking in the Available to Makeup box.

Viewing Transactions

The Sales option

You can use this dialog box to view the sales value and quantity sold for your selected product during the financial year, on a month by month basis. With a record selected:

1 From the Product Record click on Sales

2 Click Close when finished

Hot tip

To amend values for all, or a selected group of products within the Product Record, use the Global Changes option from the Tools menu.

Product Discounts

1 From the Product Record click on Discount

2 Enter Quantities for the customer to qualify for a discount and % Discount

3 Discounted value is calculated for you

4 Click Save, then Close

Use the Graph option to see how actual, budget and prior year sales values compare for particular products.

Product Activity

Details regarding adjustments of goods in and out, stock transfers, current quantities in stock, on order and allocated prove invaluable when trying to fulfil orders or analyse and track stock movement.

You can decide when you no longer wish to retain certain transactions on your system by using the Clear Stock option. This facility enables transactions to be cleared from your Product History prior to a specific date.

It is important that you understand the following terms when trying to calculate the availability of stock and to understand the product reports produced by Sage 50:

Where activities have been cleared at the month end, they will be shown as carried forward totals with a Ref. of O/BAL, usually at the top of the list.

Tp: A code to identify the type of transaction, where:

  AI   = Adjustment In

  AO   = Adjustment Out

  DI   = Damages In

  DO   = Damages Out

  GI   = Goods In (via purchase orders)

  GO   = Goods Out (via sales orders and product invoices)

  GR   = Goods Returned (via credit notes)

  MI   = Movement In (product transfer only)

  MO   = Movement Out (product transfer only)

  WO   = Write Off

To clear stock transactions, choose Period End from the Tools menu and click the Clear Stock option. Adjustments made are brought forward as opening balances, showing quantities used, in AI and MI.

Used: This is the sum of all the AO (Adjustments Out), GO (Goods Out) and MO (Movements Out) quantities for the product within the specified date range.

Cost: If the transaction line refers to an AI (Adjustment In), GI (Goods In), GR (Goods Returned), MI (Movement In) or DI (Damages In), this shows the cost price.

Sale: Where a transaction line refers to a GO (Goods Out), this shows the sales price.

Use the type code WO for recording faulty goods as write-offs.

Qty on Order: This is the product quantity which has been placed on order using the Purchase Order option, but not yet delivered.

Qty Allocated: This shows the product quantity that has been allocated to sales orders using the Sales Order Processing option.

Qty in Stock: This is the sum of all the AI (Adjustments In), MI (Movements In), GI (Goods In) and GR (Goods Received), less the quantity used for the specified period.

Qty Available: The Quantity in Stock less Quantity Allocated.

To view Activity from the Products and services window:

1 Double-click on the product required

2 From the Product Record click on Activity

3 Click here to select a different Date Range

Viewing a product's activity is also available using the Activity button from Products and services window.

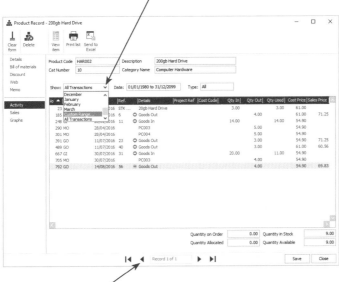

Use the Transaction Type range facility in the Date Range window to refine and speed up your search of Product activity.

4 Use previous or next if more than one product is selected

5 Click Close when finished

83

If there is a discrepancy after a stock take, just enter the stock adjustment using the Stock Take option.

Don't forget

84

Cost prices are important to the valuation of the stock, as product levels are controlled on a first in, first out basis. Always enter cost prices, therefore, to achieve accurate valuation.

Beware

You cannot use the Returns option for non-stock or service items.

Product Adjustments

The In and Out options from the Products and services window are used to record adjustments to your product's stock levels, such as when stock is received into stores, an order is returned, or stock is taken out as damaged.

The In button is used to enter any increase in a product's available stock, whilst the Out option is for recording a decrease.

To make Adjustments In

1 From the Products window, click the Adjustment in button

2 Enter the Product Code, Date and Ref, Quantity and enter the new Cost if changed

3 Click Save to store changes and Close

The Out button is used to record any miscellaneous product movements which decrease a product's available stock level and where no product invoice has been raised.

To make Adjustments Out

1 Click on Adjustment out

2 Enter Product Code, Quantity, then click Save

Product Transfers

This feature is used for increasing the In Stock quantity of Product Assemblies using components currently in stock. The Product Assemblies are set up using the Bill of Materials option (see page 80).

When using the Stock Transfers option the cost price for each Product Assembly is calculated for you by Sage 50, by adding together the cost price of each component.

To make a product transfer from the Products window:

1 Click on the Stock transfer button

2 Click on the Product Code drop-down menu button

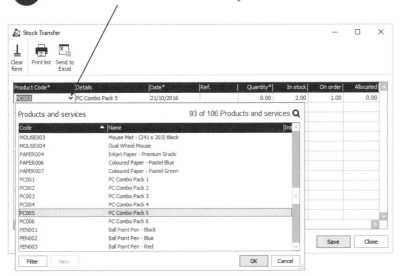

3 Select the desired Product Assembly Code and click OK

4 Check the Details and Date

5 Enter Quantity required – Sage 50 warns you if there is insufficient stock available to make the product assembly

6 Click Save to record entries or Clear form to start again

7 Click Close

You can only use a product code which has been previously set up to be a product assembly using the BOM option.

If you do not have sufficient stock of components to make up the quantity you have entered, Sage 50 will display a warning.

Check your component stock levels by clicking on the Shortfall button on the Products and services toolbar (Accounts Plus and Professional only).

Product Reports

The Stock Reports option allows you to print out a wide range of useful pre-prepared product related reports. These reports show such things as product details and movements, and will help you to keep track of what you have in stock, its financial value, etc.

Additional product reports tailored to your business needs can be created using the Report Designer (see Chapter 12). To run a Product Report:

1 From the Products and services window, click Reports

2 First, click on the required group and select a report

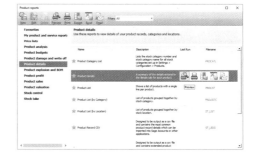

3 Click Preview to generate the report

4 Enter any required Criteria

5 Click OK to generate report

6 Click Print, then Close when done

7 Invoices

This chapter shows you how to produce invoices and credit notes for your products and services. Customers, Products and Nominal Accounts are directly linked to Invoicing, so the invoices that you produce automatically update the relevant ledgers.

The Invoicing Toolbar

This toolbar provides facilities for generating invoices, quotes, proformas and credit notes for the goods you sell and the services you provide. Ledgers can be automatically updated, transactions printed out and reports generated for analysis.

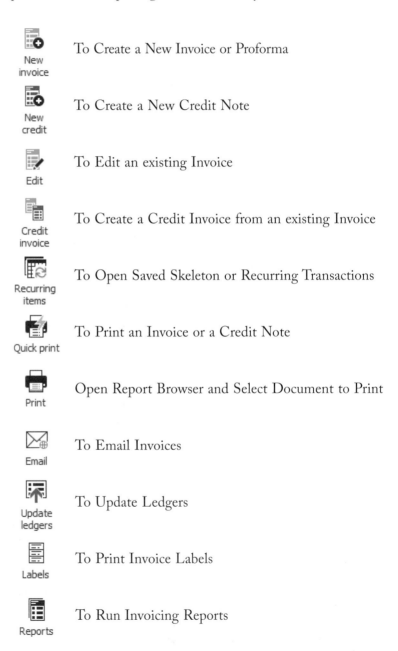

New invoice — To Create a New Invoice or Proforma

New credit — To Create a New Credit Note

Edit — To Edit an existing Invoice

Credit invoice — To Create a Credit Invoice from an existing Invoice

Recurring items — To Open Saved Skeleton or Recurring Transactions

Quick print — To Print an Invoice or a Credit Note

Print — Open Report Browser and Select Document to Print

Email — To Email Invoices

Update ledgers — To Update Ledgers

Labels — To Print Invoice Labels

Reports — To Run Invoicing Reports

Invoicing

Processing manually-generated invoices, or batch invoicing, i.e. items not generated using Sage 50, has already been referred to in Chapters 2 and 3. Briefly, Chapter 2 (Customers) explains how to log invoices and credit notes within the system after they have been produced and sent to customers. Chapter 3 (Suppliers) explains how to record the invoices and credit notes you receive from your suppliers.

Invoicing deals with Sage 50-generated invoices, of which there are two basic types. First there is the Product Invoice, which is used for invoicing customers for the products you sell. Each line of the invoice can be used for recording specific product items. Early discount settlement can be offered on these invoices and carriage charges applied.

Secondly, the Service Invoice is used to invoice customers you have provided a service for. An unlimited amount of text can be entered into the invoice, describing the services supplied. Discount settlement can be applied and carriage charges recorded.

As Sage 50 generates these invoices, all the relevant details are automatically recorded and posted for you when you are ready. For invoices where the same information is entered regularly, the Memorise option saves the invoice as a template. This template can then be recalled when required and updated with the new information, saving valuable time.

Within Invoicing is the facility to generate credit notes for your customers, where products or services, for example, have not been received or had to be returned. When these transactions are posted, the ledgers will be updated automatically.

You do, of course, need to keep track of your invoicing. Use the report facility regularly to print out a list of invoices not yet printed or posted, or to check on stock requirements or shortfalls for the invoices you have generated using this Invoicing option.

In recent versions of Sage 50, the Invoicing toolbar once again contains separate buttons for Product/Service Invoices and Credit Notes. There is now also a toolbar button that allows you to create a credit invoice directly from an existing invoice, should the whole of that invoice need to be credited to your customer, thus saving time on typing up a separate credit note.

Sage 50 generates invoice numbers in sequence, normally starting at 1. However, you can start with your own numbering system, of up to seven digits. This will be incremented for you each time a new invoice is generated.

Your Invoices remain in the Invoicing window list box until removed using the Delete option.

In the latest versions of Sage 50 Accounts, use the Credit invoice button to create a credit directly from an existing invoice.

Beware

You cannot amend a product invoice where the quantity was entered using the Sales Order Processing option.

Don't forget

As well as normal product codes, you can also enter special non-product codes:

S1 = Special product
     item with price
     and VAT amount

S2 = Special product
     item, exempt for
     VAT (Tax code T0)

S3 = Special service
     item with price
     and VAT amount

M = Message, with a
    description and
    up to two
    comment lines

The Product Invoice

To invoice your customers for the products you sell, use the New invoice option from the Invoices and credits toolbar, ensuring that the Product option is selected in the Format box. To create an Invoice, select Invoicing and credits from the navigation bar or from Modules in the menu bar and do the following:

1 Click New invoice on the Invoices and credits toolbar (see page 98). By default, Invoice and Product appear in Type and Format

2 Enter the tax point Date if different

3 Type sales Order No. if applicable

4 Enter Customer Account Code, customer details appear

5 Enter the Product Code (use the Finder button), followed by the Quantity

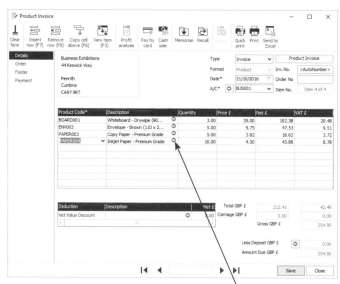

6 Repeat Step 5 for further products, clicking here if you need to edit any of the product details, then click Save

7 Click Close

Product Invoice Order Details

You can also record useful additional order details on your Invoice if necessary:

1 Click on the Order option in the navigation bar

2 Enter Delivery Address, if different, plus any Notes

3 Enter Customer Order Details, especially the Order No.

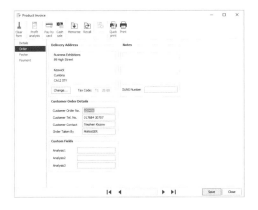

Product Invoice Footer Details

Further details, such as Carriage and Settlement Terms, go in the footer details:

1 Use Footer in the navigation bar and enter Carriage details

2 Record Settlement Terms as appropriate

3 Enter any Global detail if required

4 Click Save, then Close to finish

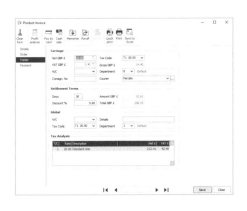

Printing an Invoice

Sage 50 gives you the option to print Invoices or Credit Notes either immediately, or at a later date. To print straight away after you have entered all of the details, instead of clicking Save (you will be asked if you wish to save the invoice) do the following:

1 From the Product Invoice window, click Print

2 Select a suitable file layout

3 Click Print to start generating the report

4 Check that the correct printer is selected in the Print window, choose Number of copies to print and click OK

5 If you wish to post the invoice and Update Ledgers, select Preview then click OK, else Cancel to print only

6 Click Close to finish

Don't forget

When using the Invoicing option to create invoices and credit notes, you can choose to either print them straight away or save a batch for printing later, using the Print option on the Invoices and credits toolbar.

Hot tip

Batching invoices or credit notes is useful if you only have one printer. Simply load the correct stationery in the printer, then print them all in one go.

Hot tip

Use the Quick print button to print an invoice without updating the ledgers.

Quick print

The Service Invoice

To invoice customers for services you provide instead of products you sell, you should generate a Service Invoice, using the New invoice button from the Invoices and credits toolbar. An unlimited amount of text can be entered to describe the services provided, and each service can be allocated to a different nominal account. Settlement discounts can be applied, as can carriage charges.

As with Product Invoices, a Service Invoice can be saved to print later or printed straight away. When printing, you have the option to update the ledgers at the same time or leave till later.

1 Click the New invoice button on the Invoices and credits toolbar and select Service in the Format field

2 Change Date if different and enter sales Order No.

3 Enter Customer Account Code – Customer details appear

4 Type service Details here and enter Net cost

5 Repeat Step 4 as necessary, then click Save

6 Click Close

To avoid having to re-create the same invoice details all the time, you can store a template using the Memorise button or simply select the required item in the invoicing window and click Duplicate.

Sage 50 warns you if a selected customer account has been marked as 'on hold' on the Customer Record.

Select a service item and click on the Edit box or Press F3 to view item details. You can then alter the Posting Details or enter a Job Reference as required.

...cont'd

Hot tip

If you make a mistake, simply click Clear form and start again.

Service Invoice Order Details

You can record useful additional Order Details on your Service Invoice if required:

1 Click on the Order option in the navigation bar

2 Enter Delivery Address and any Notes if required

3 Enter Customer Order Details, especially Order No.

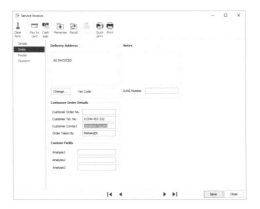

Service Invoice Footer Details

You can record details such as Carriage and Settlement Terms in the Footer details window:

1 Click on the Footer option from the navigation bar

2 Enter any Carriage details and Settlement Terms

3 Add any Global detail as required

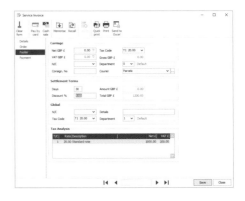

4 Click Save, then Close to finish

Hot tip

Any changes made to the delivery details are not saved back to the Customer Record.

The Skeleton Invoice

For information that is regularly repeated when creating an invoice, use the Memorise option to store the invoice as a template. You can then recall this template as and when required, and update it with the new information, thus saving valuable time and reduce keying errors.

This facility is available for both Product and Service Invoices, as well as the Product and Service Credit Notes.

1 On the Details screen enter regularly-used details only, such as Customer A/C Ref. and item Details. Omit Price

2 Click Memorise

3 Enter Filename and Description then click Save

4 When you need to use a layout, click Recall

5 Select your layout from the list and click Load

Load

Hot tip

To bring up a list of all the invoices or orders that you have saved as skeletons or recurring transactions, click the Recurring items button from the Invoices and credits toolbar.

Hot tip

A quick way to alter the date in a Date box is to use the up or down cursor keys to move through the days. Pressing Page Up or Page Down moves through the months.

Hot tip

To have Sage 50 automatically generate a transaction for you at set regular intervals, just fill in the details in the Frequency section of the Memorise window.

Product Credit Note

From time to time, goods sent to customers may be returned as faulty, past an expiry date, etc., or the customer may simply have been overcharged by mistake.

Instead of correcting the original invoice, a Product Credit Note can be issued to the Customer, detailing the amount owing to them. When your ledgers are updated, the necessary postings will be made to reflect this amendment. Do the following to create a Product Credit Note:

Hot tip

A VAT-only credit note can be raised where a customer has been invoiced and charged tax for goods which are exempt from VAT.

1 Click New credit button from the Invoices and credits toolbar and ensure that Product is in the Format field

2 Check Date and enter Order Number if relevant

3 Enter Customer Code – Customer details appear

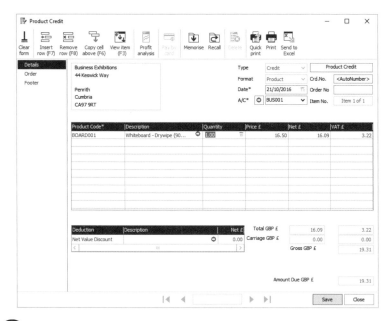

Beware

In Sage 50 you must always select the Invoice Format, i.e. Product or Service, prior to entering any product or service details. Once you begin to enter these details, the Format box turns to grey and can only be changed by discarding the invoice and starting all over again.

4 Enter the Product Code and the Quantity

5 Repeat Step 4 as required, then click Save to finish

6 Click Close

Recurring Transactions

Information that is regularly repeated when creating a Product or Service Invoice or Credit note can be stored and later recalled for use as required, or for updating. This feature is particularly useful for any recurring transactions you may have.

If the Frequency details were entered when the recurring transaction skeleton was created and memorised, Sage 50 will remind you automatically on startup if you have any outstanding transactions for processing. You can then choose to immediately post the transactions or process them at a later date as follows:

1 Click Recurring Items from the Invoicing toolbar to bring up the Memorised and Recurring Invoices window

2 Click Process

3 Remove the tick here if an entry is not to be processed, then click Process to process your recurring transactions

4 If any ticks were removed in Step 3, click No in next window

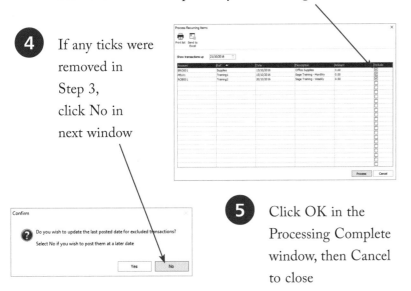

5 Click OK in the Processing Complete window, then Cancel to close

Hot tip

You can turn off the recurring transaction reminder by selecting the No Recurring Entries at Startup check box in the Bank Defaults window from the Settings menu.

97

Don't forget

Processing recurring transactions is only available in Sage 50 Accounts Plus and Professional.

Don't forget

When a recurring transaction is processed, only the invoice, purchase order or sales order is produced. You must then remember to post these items manually in order to update the ledgers or allocate any stock.

Updating your Ledgers

After creating your invoices and credit notes, the Update function is used to transfer details to the customer and nominal ledgers and, if appropriate, to amend product records.

Sage 50 gives you the option to print the update report immediately, preview it first so that you can select only certain pages for printing, or to save the report as a file. To perform an Update, do the following:

Hot tip

By regularly updating your stock records, you may find you now have enough free stock to complete outstanding sales orders.

1 From the Invoices and credits window select invoices/ credit notes for updating

2 Click the Update ledgers button to display the Output option

Beware

Always make sure you select at least one Invoice or Credit Note before using the Update function, otherwise you will be asked if you want to process ALL non-posted invoices and credit notes.

3 In the Update Ledgers window click Preview

4 Click OK to generate the update

Update Ledgers	×
OK	Output
Cancel	○ Printer ◉ Preview ○ File

5 On the report, click Print to bring up the Print dialog box, then click OK to print

6 Click Close to return to the Invoices window, then Close again

Printing for Batch Invoicing

When you created Invoices or Credit Notes, for both Product or Service, you may have decided to leave printing them until later as a batch. This can often save time when setting up file layouts and having to change the printer stationery.

For example, you may have created three Product invoices which now need printing. You would do the following:

1 From the Invoices window, select the invoices to print

2 Click Print

3 Select the Layout required

4 Click on the Preview button

5 Wait for the invoices to generate

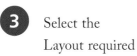

6 On the preview, click Print to bring up the Windows Print dialog box, then click OK to print

7 Close to return to the Invoices window, then Close again

You can reprint your invoices as many times as you wish.

Use Filter if you wish to print a number of invoices or credit notes that match a particular set of conditions.

Standard layouts can always be edited or new layouts created and saved as necessary. Page 144 shows you how to modify a report.

Producing Reports

The Reports option allows you to produce a wide range of reports about your product and service invoices, as well as your credit notes. Use these reports regularly to keep your business up-to-date. For example, to print an Invoices Not Posted report:

1 Click Clear then Reports from the Invoices toolbar

2 Click on the report group and select the report required

3 Click on the Preview button

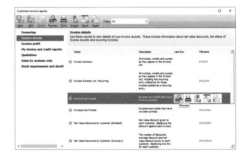

4 Wait for the Report to be generated

5 Check the report then click Print

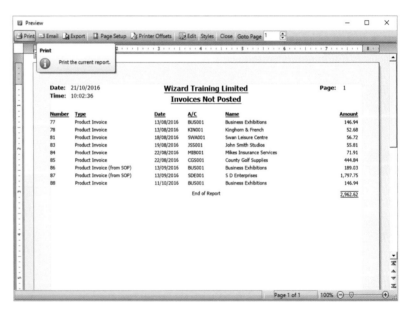

6 Click OK to print the report, then Close all windows

Hot tip

Save time: instead of searching through all your invoices for those not yet posted, use the Invoices Not Posted report instead.

Hot tip

Use the Labels button from the Invoicing toolbar to print out your invoice address labels.

8 Processing Sales Orders

Learn how to create Sales Orders and then allocate and despatch stock to these orders, as well as how to keep your stock levels up-to-date.

Sales Order Processing Toolbar

The Sales orders toolbar provides a number of features for creating a Sales Order and then controlling the allocation of stock to that order. Once you are ready to deliver the stock, you can despatch it and Sage 50 will automatically handle the stock record updates. From this toolbar you can also print Sales Orders, whilst information regarding sales order processing can be easily obtained by using the various report layouts already provided for you.

Hot tip

To quickly print out a Sales Order, simply select it from the list and click on the Quick print button on the toolbar.

Quick print

Hot tip

Use the Email button to quickly prepare and generate sales orders for emailing to customers.

Email

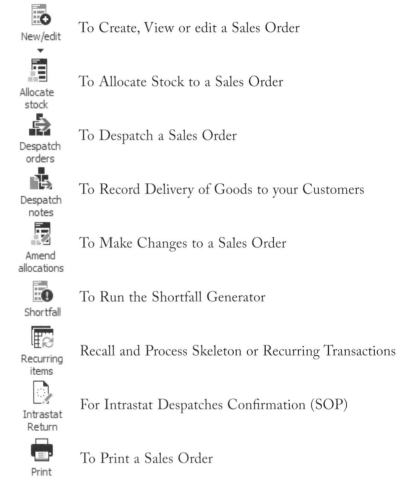

New/edit — To Create, View or edit a Sales Order

Allocate stock — To Allocate Stock to a Sales Order

Despatch orders — To Despatch a Sales Order

Despatch notes — To Record Delivery of Goods to your Customers

Amend allocations — To Make Changes to a Sales Order

Shortfall — To Run the Shortfall Generator

Recurring items — Recall and Process Skeleton or Recurring Transactions

Intrastat Return — For Intrastat Despatches Confirmation (SOP)

Print — To Print a Sales Order

Labels — To Print Sales Order Labels

Reports — To Run Sales Order Reports

The Sales Order

Sales orders can be created for the products you supply and send to customers by using the New/edit button from the Sales orders toolbar. Details from your Product records are automatically entered onto the Sales Order whilst extra details can also be added, such as a delivery address, a customer order number for future reference or a settlement discount.

To create a Sales Order, click Sales orders under Customers in the Sage 50 navigation bar, then do the following:

1 Click New/edit from the Sales orders toolbar

2 Type the required Date if different and enter Customer Account Code – Customer details appear

Use the Message box (i.e. the product code M) to add any text to the main body of the sales order, for example, 'goods supplied free'.

If you use Microsoft Outlook or Google Mail and have set up a default layout, you can email your Sales Order by clicking the Email button on the toolbar.

3 Enter the Product Code (use Finder button) and Quantity ordered

4 Repeat Step 3 for any additional products. When finished, click Save to record the Sales Order

5 Click Close

To include special one-off details against a sales item, click the Edit button (the right-facing arrow) in the Description box.

...cont'd

Sales Order Details

On the previous page you were shown how to create a Sales Order and save it immediately if no further details need to be entered. Sage 50 also gives you the option to enter additional details about the order, such as where it should be delivered if different from the main address.

From the Sales orders window, do the following to enter additional order details:

Beware

Once a Sales Order has been despatched in part or full, you cannot decrease the quantity of a product to less than the quantity despatched.

1 Select Order in the Product Sales Order navigation bar

2 Enter Delivery Address (not yet set up) if required

3 Record any Notes here

Don't forget

Sage 50 will generate an invoice and enter the Invoice Number for you automatically when the order is despatched.

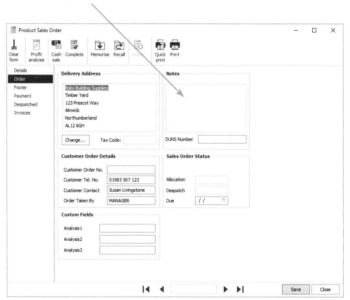

4 Enter any relevant Customer Order Details, such as a Customer Order Number or a Due despatch date

5 Click Save when finished

6 Click Close

Hot tip

If you trade physical goods with Member States of the EU, use the Intrastat button for producing trade statistics. The supply of services is excluded. Intrastat replaced customs declarations as the source of trade statistics within the EU and is closely linked with the VAT system. Use the Sage F1 Help key for more information.

Allocating Stock

Once a Sales Order has been created, stock needs allocating to it before any despatches can be recorded for the order. Using the Allocate stock option from the Sales orders toolbar allows you to automatically allocate the necessary stock needed for the selected Sales Order.

Sometimes there may be insufficient stock available to fully complete an order, in which case the order will be marked as 'Part' complete by Sage 50. There may be times when you have enough stock, but wish to only send part of the order. In this case you would use the Amend option to make changes to the order. To allocate batched Sales Orders, do the following from within the Sales orders window:

1 Click on the Sales Orders you wish to Allocate stock to

2 Click the Allocate stock button from the toolbar

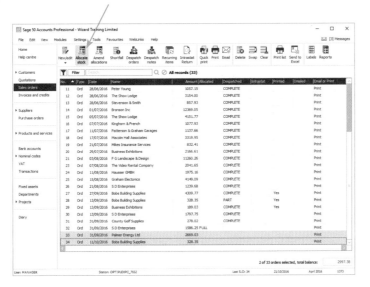

3 Click Yes to Confirm Allocation of stock

4 Note the change in Sales Order Allocated status, then click Close

Hot tip

To view a Sales Order's details, simply double-click on the item.

Don't forget

If Sage 50 cannot allocate all of the necessary stock to the order, a message box is displayed, giving suggestions and possible reasons why not.

105

Don't forget

If there is insufficient stock available for a Sales Order, the Status 'Part' appears in the Sales orders window. Fully-allocated orders display a 'Full' status.

Despatching Sales Orders

Once stock is allocated to your Sales Orders, it can be despatched at any time. The Despatch orders option also updates the product records and creates a Product Invoice for the order, as well as printing a Delivery Note.

The product invoices created through Sales Order Processing appear in the Invoicing window. These invoices can be edited, but you cannot change the quantity of the products despatched. They can then be printed and posted to the sales and nominal ledgers in the same manner as invoices created using the Invoicing option.

Don't forget

If only part of an order is despatched, Sage 50 creates an invoice for that part. This means that when the order is fully despatched, there will be more than one invoice for it.

Hot tip

Use the Shortfall option to see if you have enough stock to fulfil orders or to place purchase orders if you do not.

1 From the Sales orders window, select the required Sales Orders to despatch

2 Click the Despatch orders button from the toolbar

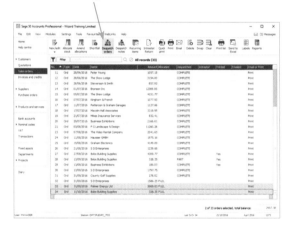

3 Click Yes to print Delivery Notes, create Invoices and Update Stock

Don't forget

Whilst you can use the Despatch orders button to quickly generate a Goods Delivery Note, remember that if you set up your GDN Options to 'Do not Generate', Sage 50 will not produce a goods despatch note.

4 Click Print Now for Delivery Notes

5 Select layout, click Preview to generate the report, then Print and Close

Amending & Printing Sales Orders

If you have allocated stock to a Sales Order, but have not yet despatched all of it, you can amend this allocation. This allows you to despatch a full order by reducing the stock allocation of another customer's order, hence perhaps reducing the number of customers waiting.

To amend the allocation of stock on a Sales Order

1 Select the order from the Sales orders window and click the Amend allocations button

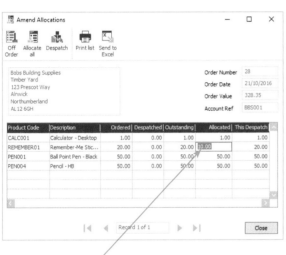

2 Amend the allocation as necessary

3 Click Close and note change in status from Full to Part

Printing Batched Orders

1 Select orders for printing and click Print

2 Choose layout and click the Preview button

3 Click Print, then Close

When you amend the allocation of stock to a Sales Order, the allocated status of the order in the Sales orders window may change to either Full, Part or even no status at all.

Remember that you can raise an invoice even if you have a negative stock situation.

107

By batching your orders, you can print them all out together after setting up the printer with sales order stationery.

Sales Orders Reports

Sage 50 provides you with a large variety of reports to help you run the Sales Order side of your business. For example, you have the facility to print a picking list for your warehouse from a particular order or the Sales Order Shortage report to show you any shortfalls in the stock.

These reports are generated from the information entered when you created a Sales Order. To generate, for example, a Sales Order Picking List:

Hot tip

Regularly use the Sales Orders to be Invoiced report for keeping your invoicing up-to-date.

Hot tip

To check how many despatched orders have gone out for a particular time period, use the Despatched Sales Orders report and apply the Order Date Criteria.

Hot tip

Use the Labels button from the Sales orders toolbar to quickly print out Sales Order Addresses or Stock labels.

1 From the Sales orders window, click the Reports button

2 Click the group and select required layout

3 Click on Preview to generate the report

4 Enter Criteria, i.e. Order Date range

5 Click OK to complete the report

6 Click Print, then OK

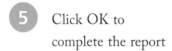

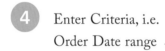

9 Purchase Orders

Create and print Purchase Orders to send to your suppliers. You will be shown how to monitor orders raised and record deliveries received, as well as produce reports to help track them.

The PO Processing Toolbar

From the Purchase orders toolbar you can create and print purchase orders as well as make amendments to orders you have already created. You have facilities for recording deliveries and producing useful reports about your Purchase Orders, such as a report indicating orders that have been delivered in part or full, or orders that are still outstanding.

Hot tip

To quickly print out a Purchase Order, simply select it from the list and click on the Quick print button on the toolbar.

New/edit

To Create, View or Edit a Purchase Order

Place orders

To put a Purchase Order 'on order'

Receive deliveries

To Record Purchase Order Deliveries

Received note

To Complete a Goods Received Note

Amend deliveries

To Make Changes to a Purchase Order

Update ledgers

To Automatically Update the Purchase Ledger

Recurring items

Recall and Process Skeleton or Recurring Transactions

Intrastat Return

For Intrastat Arrivals Confirmation (POP)

Print

To Print a Purchase Order

Labels

To Print Purchase Order Labels

Reports

To Run Purchase Order Reports

Hot tip

Use the Email button to quickly prepare Purchase Orders for emailing to your suppliers.

Email

Creating a Purchase Order

To record order details of any products you buy from a supplier, use the New/edit Order button from the Purchase orders toolbar. Details entered straight onto the Purchase Order screen are taken directly from the product records for you by Sage 50.

You can also include additional details, such as delivery address or any settlement discount given to you by your supplier, to the order. To create a Purchase Order, first select Purchase orders under Suppliers in the Sage 50 navigation bar, then follow these steps:

If a reorder quantity has been set up on the Product Record, this value is entered automatically for you in the Quantity field.

1 Click the New/edit button from the Purchase orders toolbar

2 Check Date and enter Supplier Account Code

3 Supplier details appear here

You can increase but not decrease the quantity for any Purchase Order you have already despatched, whether in full or part.

4 Enter the Product Code (use the Finder button) and Quantity

5 Repeat Step 4 for additional products and click Save when finished

For non-payment products use the product code M.

6 Click Close

Entering Purchase Order Details

You may need to record further details on your Purchase Order, such as delivery details, carriage costs, settlement terms, supplier contact or the name of the person who took your order.

Sage 50 lets you do this through the Order or Footer options. From the Purchase order window, do the following to enter additional order details:

1 Click on Order in the Purchase Order navigation bar

2 Enter Delivery Address if required

3 Record any Notes you wish to add here

4 You can change who took the order here

5 Enter any relevant Supplier Order Details, such as an Order or Telephone Number

6 Click Save when all details have been entered

7 Click Close

Hot tip

To edit an existing Purchase Order you can simply double-click on it in the Purchase orders list window.

Hot tip

Save your Purchase Order as a Skeleton if you use these details regularly.

Hot tip

Use the Footer option to record any Carriage or Settlement terms or click on Deliveries to view delivery information.

Placing Orders 'on order'

Once a Purchase Order has been created, it has to be placed 'on order' before any deliveries can be recorded for it. The Sage 50 program then updates each Product Record with the new order details accordingly.

Use the Place orders option to automatically place a single or batch of Purchase Orders 'on order', as follows:

1 From the Purchase orders window, highlight all orders you wish to place 'on order' by clicking on them

2 Click on the Place orders button from the toolbar

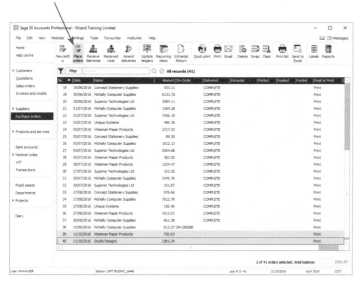

3 Click No to print a copy of the Purchase Order later, else Yes to print now

4 Click Yes to place the selected items 'on order'

5 Note that items are now ON-ORDER, then click Close

Use Filter to refine the list to only the orders you wish to work with.

To avoid costly mistakes, always check that the status of an order shows ON-ORDER after going through the process of placing it on order.

You can also put Purchase Orders 'on order' from within the Amend deliveries option.

Recording Deliveries

To automatically record the complete delivery of stock for Purchase Orders, use the Receive deliveries option from the Purchase orders toolbar.

You should remember that Sage 50 always assumes that you have taken full delivery of all the products needed to complete the selected Purchase Order. If a part delivery needs recording, you must do so using the Amend function (see page 116).

To record Purchase Order deliveries do the following:

1 From the Purchase orders window select any orders you wish to mark as received

2 Click on Receive deliveries from the toolbar

3 Click Yes to Confirm delivery and update stock records, then choose whether to print a Goods Received Note (GRN) now or later

4 Note the Purchase Order now displays as COMPLETE, then if finished, click Close

Beware

When you use the Delivery option it is assumed that you have taken full delivery of all items on the Purchase Order. Note that the Delivery record cannot be altered later.

Don't forget

You can only record deliveries for orders which you have already put 'on order'.

Don't forget

Sage 50 automatically makes adjustments for each product that you mark as delivered.

Processing Purchases Manually

To check and keep track of your Purchase Orders, use the Amend deliveries option. In this window you can manually place them 'on order' (thus updating On-Order levels for the appropriate product records), record full or part deliveries of stock against each order and cancel orders.

Placing a Purchase Order 'on order' manually

You have already learned how to place Purchase Orders 'on order' using the Place orders button (page 113). However, Sage 50 also allows you to do this manually as follows:

1 From the Purchase orders window, select the Purchase Order you require

2 Click Amend deliveries to bring up the Amend window

3 Click on the Order button to place 'on order'

4 Note the order now looks normal and the full order quantity appears in This Delivery

5 Click Close

You can cancel a Purchase Order which is 'on order' using the Amend option. Just click Off Order to mark it as cancelled, click Order to put it back 'on order'.

If you use Microsoft Outlook or Google Mail and have set up a default layout, you can email your Purchase Order by clicking on Email on the toolbar.

You can use the Received note button to quickly generate a Goods Received Note, but remember that if you set up your GRN Options in Invoice and Order Defaults to 'Do not Generate', Sage 50 will not produce a goods received note.

Recording Deliveries Manually

You use Receive deliveries from the Purchase orders toolbar only when you have received full delivery of an order.

If you wish to record part deliveries, then you must use the Amend deliveries option, though you can still record full deliveries this way as well, should you need to. To record a Purchase Order part delivery, follow these steps:

Don't forget

If the order is not 'on order' or has been cancelled, Sage 50 reminds you to place the Purchase Order 'on order' to enable you to record the delivery.

1 From the Purchase orders window, select the order you wish to record a part delivery for

2 Click on the Amend deliveries button from the toolbar

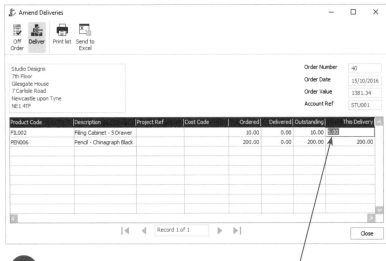

Hot tip

Use the Received Notes button from the Purchase Order Processing toolbar to quickly produce Goods Received Notes.

3 Enter part quantity received in the This Delivery column

4 Click on the Deliver button to update your Product Record details

5 Click Yes to confirm updating of order

Hot tip

Use the Amend deliveries option if you wish to record part deliveries for your Purchase Orders.

6 Click Close to finish and note that the status is now PART delivered

Printing Batched Orders

Rather than print your Purchase Orders straight away, you may have chosen to save them until later. This is useful if you only have one printer and need to change the stationery. When you are ready, you can then print the orders out in batches.

As with all the printing facilities in Sage 50, you can send the Purchase Order direct to the printer, save it as a file or first preview it on the screen. To preview an order and then print it, do the following:

1 From the Purchase orders window, select the order or orders for printing

2 Click on the Print button from the toolbar

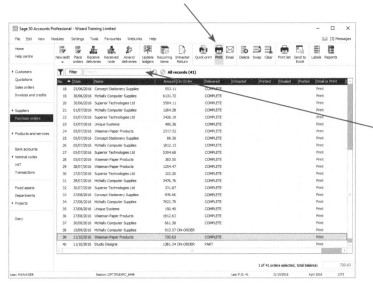

To print a specific selection of Purchase Orders, use the Search facility.

3 Select required Purchase Order layout

4 Click Preview button

5 On the preview, click Print then click OK

6 Click Close

If your business trades physical goods with Member States of the EU, use the Intrastat button for producing trade statistics.

117

Purchase Order Reports

Standard reports have already been set up for you to display any outstanding Purchase Orders, or orders which have already been delivered or part delivered. These reports can be previewed on screen, sent to your printer or saved to a file for previewing or printing later.

To generate a report of any Purchase Orders not yet delivered or part delivered, do the following:

1 From the Purchase orders toolbar, click Reports

2 Select required layout and click on the Preview button

3 Wait while the report starts generating

4 Enter Criteria, if any applies

5 Click OK to generate report

6 Click Print to send to printer, then OK and Close

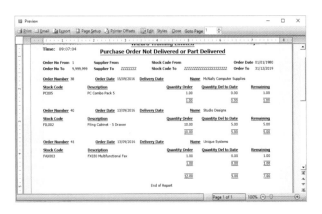

10 Financial Reporting

Generate financial reports so you can analyse your business transactions. This includes the Trial Balance, Profit and Loss, the Balance Sheet, the Budget and Prior Year reports, plus how to produce a VAT Return and make a submission online.

Financial Reporting Toolbars

From these toolbars you can generate all the financial reports you need, to not only keep track of how your business is doing financially, but also trace back and find out when certain transactions took place. The Audit Trail is particularly useful, as it is a complete record of your transaction activities, whilst the VAT function gives you all the features you need to produce accurate VAT Returns.

Previously, Financials was a single module but in the latest Sage 50 versions, these facilities are distributed and included in modules more appropriate to the function. The Audit Trail report is in the Transactions module, the Trial Balance and Profit and Loss reports, etc., are in Nominal codes, whilst VAT is now a separate module. For simplicity, the various toolbars are shown together on this page.

Audit trail report To Produce the Audit Trail Report

Trial balance Run the Trial Balance Report

Profit & loss To Produce the Profit and Loss Report

Balance sheet To Produce the Balance Sheet Report

Ratio Run the Quick Ratio Report

Variances To Produce the Budget Report

Prior year Run the Prior Year Report

VAT Return To Produce a VAT Return

VAT audit To Check for possible Audit or VAT Anomalies

Reports To Run Financial Reports

The Audit Trail

The Audit Trail records details about transactions entered into the system, and it is a very useful source of information for checking and cross-referencing. It may also be referred to when auditing your accounts.

The Audit Trail button gives you a range of Audit Trail formats providing brief, summary or fully-detailed reports which can be previewed, printed directly or saved as a file for use later. A report of deleted transactions can also be printed. Use the Audit Trail regularly to ensure your transactions are being recorded accurately.

To view the Audit Trail:

1 From the Sage 50 navigation bar, click Transactions to bring up the Transactions window displaying the Audit Trail

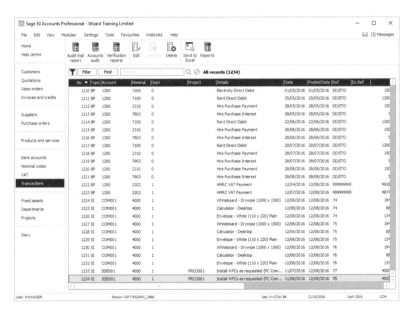

2 Use both horizontal and vertical arrow buttons and scroll bars to examine all transaction details

3 When you have finished examining the Audit Trail, click Close

Deleted transactions always appear in red.

Transaction codes used in the Audit Trail are explained on page 49.

When you clear transactions from the Audit Trail, Sage 50 brings them forward as opening balances in your financial reports.

...cont'd

To print the Audit Trail report

The Criteria box options vary according to the type of Audit Trail report you have selected.

1 From the Transactions toolbar, click Audit trail report

2 Select Audit Trail Type, e.g. Brief

3 Check Output is set to Preview and click Run to continue

4 Enter required Criteria

5 Click here to Exclude Deleted Transactions from the report

You can choose to exclude deleted transactions from your reports and instead, print them as a separate report later.

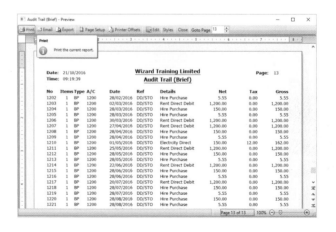

6 Click OK to produce the report

7 If you want to print the report, click Print and OK, then close all windows

Make sure you print your Audit Trail reports at least every month to use for reference purposes.

The Trial Balance

This report displays a simple listing of the current balances in all your nominal ledger accounts. It shows total values for both the debit and credit entries for all the nominal codes containing a balance value.

Since Sage 50 controls the double-entry accounting for you, the debit and credit columns will always balance. To produce the Trial Balance report, select Nominal codes and do the following:

1 From the Nominal codes toolbar click Trial balance to bring up the Print Output window

2 Ensure Preview is selected and click Run

3 Select period required here

4 Click OK to generate the Trial Balance

You can run this report for any month as it proves a valuable source of data for your management information.

123

5 If you want to print the report, click Print and OK, then close all windows

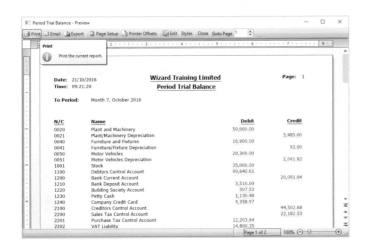

Profit & Loss Report

This important financial report shows whether your business is trading at a profit over a particular period of time. The report can be produced for the current month or a range of consecutive months within your current financial year.

The balances of each of your income and expenditure nominal ledger accounts appear on the standard Profit and Loss report. These categories, i.e. Sales, Purchases, Direct Expenses and Overheads, are grouped together and display a sub-total. The Gross Profit/(Loss) and Net Profit/(Loss) amount is also shown.

Don't forget

Balances are posted before the start of the financial year and so will appear as a prior year adjustment on the balance sheet, not on the Profit and Loss Report sheet.

Hot tip

Use the Comparative Profit & Loss button for a report comparing actual profit and loss values for a period with the budget and/or prior year values.

Comparative profit & loss

Beware

Unless you have set up your own layout, ensure you choose the Default Layout of Accounts in Step 4, otherwise you will not generate the correct report.

1 From the Nominal codes toolbar, click the Profit & loss button

2 Ensure Preview is selected and click Run

3 Select period required here

4 Select Default Layout of Accounts (1) then click OK

5 If you want to print the report, click Print and OK, then close all windows

The Balance Sheet

The Balance Sheet shows the financial position of a business at a particular time by outlining its assets (what it owns) and its liabilities (what it owes). There are two main types of assets: fixed and current. Fixed assets are long-term and have material substance such as premises, equipment and vehicles; whilst current assets are continually changing and include stock, debtors, bank, cash accounts, etc.

The Balance Sheet shows the fixed and current assets, as well as the liabilities. By adding together the assets and subtracting the liabilities, the Balance Sheet shows the Capital, or net assets.

1 Click Balance sheet from the Nominal codes toolbar

2 Select Preview and click Run

3 Select period required here

4 Select Default Layout of Accounts (1) then click OK

5 Click Print and OK, then close all windows

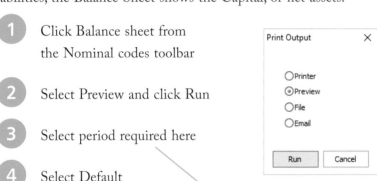

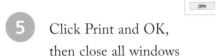

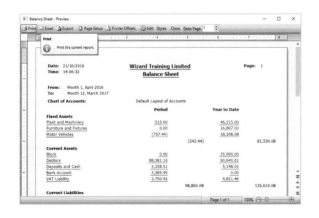

Hot tip

Use the Balance Sheet regularly to give a summary of your current financial position.

Don't forget

The difference between assets and liabilities is referred to as the company's net assets (or net worth).

Don't forget

Liabilities consist of both current and long-term. Current liabilities are amounts owing at the Balance Sheet date and due for repayment within 12 months or less, e.g. trade creditors. Long-term liabilities are amounts due for repayment in more than 12 months, e.g. a bank loan.

Quick Ratio Report

Using the data available within the system, the Quick Ratio Report allows you to see the current liquidity position of the business. This type of information is necessary for making financial decisions about future investments or developments, and will be required by a number of different parties, for example: management, bank managers and shareholders.

These Ratio Reports highlight both the strengths and the weaknesses in the financial position of your business. Credit and debit balances are compared to show the net balance using previously set up nominal account codes. You can edit the report to include other nominal accounts you wish to compare.

To view or edit the Quick Ratio report

1 From the Nominal codes window, click the Ratio button

2 To edit the nominal accounts, use Finder button to select Nominal Code required

3 Click Print, then Run in the Print Output window

4 Select Period

5 Click OK

Hot tip

Use the Quick Ratio Report to see the immediate financial position of your company. This is useful when you are considering future investments etc.

Hot tip

Click the Save button to quickly store a handy Quick Ratio report for future reference.

The Budget Report

The Budget Report displays the current values in your purchases, sales, direct expenses and overhead account codes for the months you select and the year-to-date. Use this report to see how your business actually traded compared with the monthly budget you set against the nominal ledger accounts for the chosen months and the year-to-date.

1. Click Variances from the Nominal codes toolbar

2. Ensure Preview is selected and click Run

3. In the Criteria box enter the from and to Period required

4. Select Default Layout of Accounts (1)

5. Click OK to generate the report

6. Click Print and OK, then close all windows

Print Output ✕

- ○ Printer
- ◉ Preview
- ○ File
- ○ Email

[Run] [Cancel]

Criteria for Budget Report ✕

Criteria Values
Enter the values to use for the criteria in this report

| Period | Between (Inclusive) ▼ | 1: April 2016 ▼ | and | 12: March 2017 ▼ |
| Chart of Accounts | Is ▼ | 1: Default Layout of / ▼ | | |

Preview a sample report for a specified number of records or transactions (0 for all) 0

Help   OK   Cancel

Hot tip

You can amend your nominal account Budget values at any time by using the Global Changes feature from the Tools menu.

Hot tip

When you run a year end, Sage 50 offers you the option to move the actual monthly values for the year just ended to the budgets for the coming year. This sets the budget values to be what really happened in each month of the year just ended. You can also add a percentage increase to your budget values to reflect any anticipated rise in sales, purchases, costs, etc. for the coming year.

127

The VAT Return

For businesses that need to submit VAT Return forms to HM Revenue and Customs, Sage 50 provides all the features to enable you to do this quickly and accurately, calculating both input and output tax for you from the information you have entered over the period. This is one of the prime reasons for always keeping accurate accounts.

Input tax is the VAT you are charged on your business purchases and expenses. Output tax is the VAT your business charges on its taxable supplies or services. Since Value Added Tax is a tax charged to the final consumer, a business needs to calculate what input tax can be reclaimed and how much output tax needs paying to Revenue and Customs. This is the purpose of the document called the VAT Return.

You have the facility to set up 100 tax codes, but on installation Sage 50 sets the standard UK and EC VAT rates for you, so you will probably not have to change anything. The default is set to the standard rate T1, presently at 20.00%, whilst others you may need are T0 (zero-rated) and T9 (transactions not involving VAT).

Within the nominal ledger there are three accounts, namely Sales Tax Control account (2200), Purchase Tax Control account (2201) and VAT liability account (2202). An accumulated total appears in the Sales account for the output tax charged to your customers, whilst another accumulated total appears in the Purchase account for the input tax charged to your business.

When your VAT Return is due, enter the correct date range into the system and the program will calculate the difference between the input and output tax and will inform you of the net VAT due to either the Revenue and Customs or to yourselves.

After reconciling your VAT Return, VAT on the Sales and Purchases Control accounts for this VAT period need to be transferred to the VAT Liability nominal account. When a bank payment to the Revenue and Customs is made or received, the VAT Liability account is cleared, leaving a zero balance.

If you have internet access, Sage 50 lets you make your VAT submission and payment online as detailed on page 131, though you will first need to obtain your e-Submissions Credentials. Sage Help on VAT e-Submissions shows you how to do this and has a link direct to the HMRC website.

Don't forget

Before reconciling your VAT transactions, you should always back up your data files. Reconciling your transactions sets a flag against each transaction so it is automatically excluded from subsequent VAT Returns.

Hot tip

The Audit Trail VAT column shows whether a transaction is reconciled or not:

- R = reconciled

- N = unreconciled

- - (a hyphen) or – (a dash) = a non-VAT transaction

...cont'd

To produce your VAT Return

1 From the Sage navigation bar, click VAT then VAT Return to bring up the VAT Return window showing zero totals

2 Enter the date range for the VAT Return

3 Click Calculate VAT return to calculate totals for this return. You will be informed if any unreconciled transactions are found

Don't forget

Ensure all transactions have been fully reconciled and the Audit Trail checked before running your VAT Return.

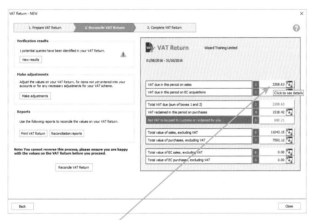

4 Click on a VAT total for a breakdown

5 Double-click on a Tax Code for a transaction breakdown

Hot tip

Use the Validation reports to quickly check for possible Audit or VAT anomalies before running the VAT Return.

6 Close each window to return to VAT Return

7 Click Print, Run and OK

8 Click Reconcile VAT Return

...cont'd

Transferring VAT liability

Having prepared and printed the VAT Return you are ready to transfer your VAT liability to the Nominal Ledger and make your VAT submission.

Don't forget

Note that Sage 50 already has the following tax rates set up:

T0 = zero rated transactions

T1 = standard rate

T2 = exempt transactions

T4 = sales to customers in EC

T7 = zero rated purchases from suppliers in EC

T8 = standard rated purchases from suppliers in EC

T9 = transactions not involving VAT

130

1 First, ensure the VAT Return shows confirmation that it has been reconciled

2 The right-hand side of the VAT Return window has been completed for you by Sage 50

3 Check the posting details in the VAT transfer area are correct, change the date if necessary then click on Post Journal

4 Confirmation appears when VAT transfer is complete

5 Select Nominal codes

6 Check the Sales and Purchase Tax Control account entries reflect the above, as should the VAT liability

VAT e-Submissions

Since April 2010 all large and medium sized companies, most small traders and all newly registered VAT traders have been required to file their VAT returns online and pay electronically; paper submissions no longer being accepted.

If you didn't choose to set up VAT e-Submission during the setting of your VAT Preferences, you can do so now, as follows:

1 Visit the HMRC website and obtain your e-Submission Credentials

2 From the Sage 50 menu click Settings, Company Preferences, then VAT

3 Enter your Credentials and Contact Details

4 Enter HMRC Bank Account details here

5 Click OK to save

Don't forget

You can only make an online VAT submission for a return whose status is Pending or Partial. For a payment, the status must be Submitted but Not Paid.

131

Making an online VAT submission

1 From the VAT Return click Submit online

2 Once submitted, to pay or reclaim from HMRC, check payment details and Date then click Post Bank Payment

Financial Reports

Sage 50 offers a wide range of Financial Reports that provide management information to enable effective decision-making, planning and forecasting.

A considerable number of reports are set up at installation time, but many can be customised if required for your business by changing the appearance of the layout, the font type or by adding/removing certain text. Refer to Chapter 12 for more details. To generate a report, do the following:

Don't forget

With Sage 50 you can calculate profit and loss for the current month or for any range of consecutive months within your current financial year.

1 From the Transactions toolbar, click Reports

2 Click on the appropriate folder and select the report layout

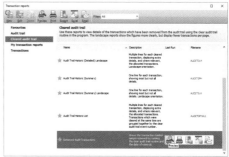

3 Click on the Preview button

4 Wait as the report is generated

Don't forget

The grouping and positioning of nominal codes on the Financial Reports is determined by the relevant Chart of Accounts in use.

5 Enter Criteria and click OK to complete the report, then Print

To Verify System

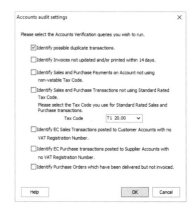

1 Click the Accounts audit button from the Transactions toolbar

2 Click OK to run the selected checks

Don't forget

Information used for creating Financial Reports is taken from the Actuals column in the Nominal Ledger Record.

11 Fixed Assets

Learn all about Fixed Asset

Records and how to view

the value of all your assets.

The Fixed Assets Toolbar

This toolbar features options for creating Fixed Asset Records and setting up the method of depreciation, performing valuation of Fixed Assets and the generation of your Fixed Asset reports.

 Create a Fixed Asset Record

New

 To Edit a Fixed Asset Record

Edit

 Duplicate a Fixed Asset Record

Duplicate

 To Report on Asset Valuation

Valuation

 To Dispose of a Fixed Asset

Disposal

 To run Fixed Asset Reports

Reports

Note:

An alternative to using the Fixed assets button on the navigation bar is to use the Modules menu, as follows:

1 On the Sage 50 menu bar, click Modules

2 Click on Fixed assets to bring up the Fixed assets window

The Fixed assets window is once again available from the navigation bar in new versions of Sage 50 Accounts.

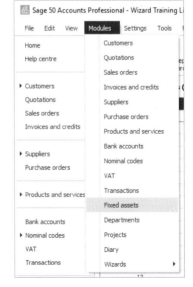

Recording your Fixed Assets

Fixed Assets are items such as office equipment, buildings, machinery, etc., owned by the business. Their depreciation is an expense and can be offset against profits.

However, before recording Fixed Asset information, it is important that the correct method and rate of depreciation be decided upon and applied consistently. Different classes of Fixed Assets are often depreciated at different rates, for example, office furniture may be depreciated at a different rate to motor vehicles.

Sage 50 offers the choice of three depreciation methods: Straight Line, Reducing Balance and Write Off. For the Straight Line method, the asset is depreciated by a fixed percentage (calculated from the original Cost Price of the asset) every month until the asset is reduced to zero. For the Reducing Balance method, the asset is depreciated, again monthly, by a fixed percentage, but this time the percentage is applied to the new book value of the asset.

The last method, Write Off depreciation, makes one last posting to depreciate the remaining value of the asset.

When ready to enter your fixed assets for the first time, you will notice that the Fixed Assets window is empty. As soon as Fixed Asset Records are entered, they will be displayed one record per line. To bring up the Fixed Assets window and view details:

1 Click Fixed assets on the Sage 50 navigation bar

2 Double-click on a record or select a record and click the Edit button to view details

3 Click Close when done to return to the Fixed assets window

Have the following information ready before entering your Fixed Asset Records: purchase date of asset and cost price, depreciation method and rate, depreciation balance sheet and depreciation profit and loss nominal codes.

To delete an Asset, just highlight it in the Fixed Assets window, then click the Delete button.

...cont'd

Adding Fixed Asset Records

The first time you use the Assets option, the Fixed assets window will be empty. To add a Fixed Asset record, have all the necessary information to hand, then do the following:

1 From the Fixed assets toolbar click the New button

2 Enter a unique code to identify asset, no spaces allowed

3 Type a Description and a Serial Number, plus Location if relevant to this asset

You cannot save a new Fixed Asset Record unless the nominal ledger posting details have all been entered.

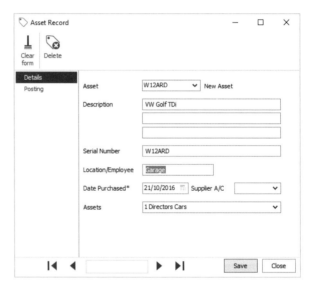

Use the Tab key to move from one data entry box to the next.

4 Enter the Date Purchased

5 If the asset was bought from one of your current Suppliers, select Supplier A/C

6 For reporting purposes select Assets category from the list

Although you have now entered all of the initial details for this asset, before you can save this new record you still need to enter the appropriate nominal ledger posting details. This is explained on pages 137-138.

Fixed Asset Depreciation

The Posting option in the Fixed Asset Record window is used for entering the necessary nominal ledger posting details. Then, when you run the Month End/Year End depreciation posting routines, asset depreciation will be added to the appropriate account code as an expense to your business and will be shown on the Balance Sheet and Profit and Loss Report.

There are four depreciation accounts already set up in the Balance Sheet of the nominal ledger by Sage 50. Every time an asset is depreciated, the amount of depreciation is posted as a credit posting. Codes include 0021 (Plant/Machinery Depreciation), 0031 (Office Equipment Depreciation), 0041 (Furniture/Fixture Depreciation) and 0051 (Motor Vehicles Depreciation).

Similarly, four depreciation accounts are already set up for you in the Profit and Loss section of the nominal ledger. Every time an asset is depreciated, the value of that depreciation is added to the account code as an expense to the company (debit posting). Codes include 8001 (Plant/Machinery Depreciation), 8002 (Furniture/Fitting Depreciation), 8003 (Vehicle Depreciation) and 8004 (Office Equipment Depreciation).

You need to enter the annual rate of depreciation. For the Straight Line method, the value entered will be divided by 12 to calculate the monthly depreciation. For example, to depreciate an asset completely over five years using the Straight Line method, the Depreciation Rate would be 20%, depreciating at 1.666% monthly until after five years the book value is zero. So, for an item costing £15,000, a depreciation value of £250 would be posted for a term of 60 months.

Where Book Value details are required, then enter the current book value. If the asset is brand new, this should be the same as the Cost Price. If an asset has already been depreciated, then enter the cost price minus depreciation. If the Reducing Balance method was selected, the Book Value will be used to calculate the depreciation amount. Sage 50 will then automatically reduce this value by the depreciation amount when the month end procedure is run.

The Fixed Asset option does not post depreciation for you, it only records the asset and current value. Use the Month End option to automatically make any depreciation postings.

Once you have saved a record, the depreciation method can only ever be changed to Write Off.

To record a Fixed Asset Disposal, simply click on the Disposal button on the Fixed assets toolbar and follow the step-by-step Wizard.

Depreciation and Valuation

Setting up a Fixed Asset depreciation posting

1 From the Fixed Asset Record select the Posting option

2 Select Department, where appropriate

3 Enter the nominal ledger Balance Sheet account code and the nominal ledger Profit and Loss account code

From the Fixed assets window, click the Valuation button to quickly check the totals for cost, current book value and the amount of depreciation that has taken place so far on all of your asset records.

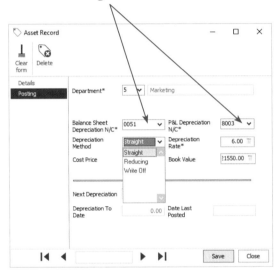

4 Select Depreciation Method and enter annual percentage Depreciation Rate

5 Enter Cost Price (Net) and the current Book Value then click Save to store the details

Valuation of Fixed Assets

To see details about the current value of your assets including total cost, previous total depreciation and total current book value:

1 From the Fixed assets window, click the Valuation button on the toolbar to bring up the Asset Valuation window

2 When finished, click Close

Don't forget

Sage 50 lets you save both non-depreciating assets as well as depreciating assets.

138

12 The Report Designer

Lay out a report, add filters,

calculations and criteria.

The Report Designer

When you first install Sage 50, you can immediately generate and print all of the reports and stationery to suit most business needs. If you use stationery supplied by Sage, the data should fit in the pre-printed stationery forms without adjustment.

There will be occasions, though, when you need a new report not already supplied, or you need to modify an existing one to suit your specific needs. The Report Designer lets you do all of this to meet any specific requirements you may have.

The Report Designer included as an integral part of Sage 50 is actually a complete Windows application on its own. The Designer has its own Title Bar, Menu Bar, and Desktop area on which you can open multiple document windows. Each document window can hold an entirely separate layout file, which means you can work on several layouts at once, if you wish. You can also convert old Report Designer layouts from earlier versions to the new format. To run the Report Designer, do the following:

1 On the Sage menu bar select Tools, then Report Designer

2 Double-click on a folder for a list of existing layouts

Hot tip

For more details about the Report Designer simply press F1.

Hot tip

Use the Report Designer to quickly create or modify your own reports, stationery layouts, letters and labels.

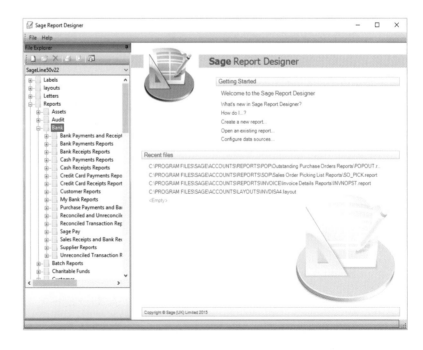

140

Creating a New Report

The following example shows you how to create a Customer Balance and Credit List for a single customer or a range of customers using the Report Wizard. The report contains the Customer's account reference, company name and account balance, together with their credit limit. The report is sorted to show the customer with the lowest balance first. The report also displays a balance total.

When the wizard is finished, the Report Designer appears with the new report or layout open ready for you to work on or preview.

1 Click File, New, Report from the Report Designer menu

2 Select the Customer option and click Next

3 Double-click on a field table and select the variables required from the list

To save time you can double-click the required variable to copy it to the Report Variables view.

4 Click Add (▶) to copy to Report Variables view

5 Repeat selection for all required variables and click Next

6 Group on NAME and click Next

7 Select SALES_LEDGER.ACCOUNT_REF for the Sort

Use the Favourites option in the Report Browser to access the most frequently used reports.

8 Click Add, confirm Ascending and click Next

...cont'd

Only numeric variables will be listed to Total on when designing a report.

9 Select SALES_LEDGER.CREDIT_LIMIT from Totals

10 Click Remove (◄)

11 Click Next

12 Remove all but Customer Ref and Transaction Date from the Selected criteria window

Criteria State can be set to Disabled, Enabled or Preset. This controls the Criteria screen that appears prior to running the report.

13 Set both criteria to Enabled in the State column

14 Click Next

15 Enter a report name then choose a template if required and click Finish to generate the layout

Should you ever need to remove all the Total Variables, simply click the << Remove All button.

The Report Designer now generates the appropriate report layout for you. You will be able to see how the layout is divided into sections, i.e. Page Header, Details, Page Footer, etc. Remember though, that depending upon your own options and settings, the initial layout may differ to that shown. For example, you may have to manually enable Criteria, add a Page Header or Footer, etc.

If the layout is not as required, you can modify the report later. First, you need to check that it provides the information you require by running a report preview.

142

Previewing your Report

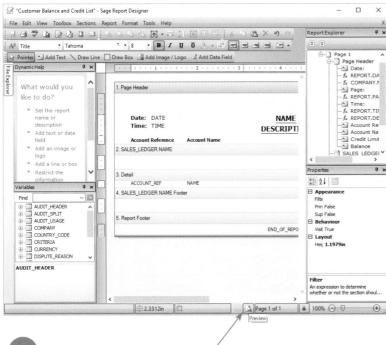

Hot tip

If your new report has no Page Header or Footer, remove the tick from the Use Data Path for Reports option in Company Preferences and try creating the report again.

1 Click Preview to run your new report

2 Enter Criteria details here

3 Click OK to run the report

Hot tip

To speed up report design you can cut and paste groups of variables between two reports.

4 To save, select Save As from File menu, enter a filename and click OK

5 To close, click on File and Exit

Beware

Be careful not to overwrite any existing reports. They may be useful to you later.

Modifying an Existing Report

The Report Designer lets you modify existing report layout files and default reports supplied with the program. These will, however, need saving under a new filename.

As an example, you can modify the report just created and saved to include only those customers having a balance greater than £1000. This is called a filter, which is embedded in the report layout. Assuming you saved your new report under Customers, to make this change it is easier to start from the Customers option:

To remove your company's name and address from all your layout files, select Company Preferences from the Settings menu on the Sage 50 toolbar. Click on the Reporting tab and deselect the Print Address on Stationery check box, then click OK.

1 From the Customers toolbar, click on the Reports button

2 Open the correct group, select your report and click Edit

3 Click Report, Filters then Use Advanced Filter

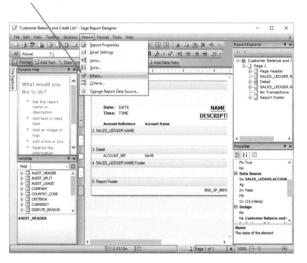

144

You can edit some Fixed Reports and save them to a new filename. The original report remains unchanged and your new report is added to the list.

4 Double-click SALES_LEDGER.BALANCE here

5 Type >1000 here, then OK

6 Click OK, Preview and Save

When you are familiar with using filters, save time by typing filter details directly into the Modify Filter window instead of using the Expression Editor.

13 Opening Balances

This chapter explains opening balances and how to enter opening balances for your customer, supplier, nominal and bank accounts as well as for your products.

Print off a copy of the Opening Balances checklist to guide you during set up.

Don't forget

Posted Opening Balances for your customers and suppliers are displayed in the Trial Balance Report, which needs clearing before entering any Opening Balances for your nominal ledger accounts, bank accounts and products.

Hot tip

Note that these are the Nominal Codes used in the Trial Balance:

1100 = Debtors Control Account

2100 = Creditors Control Account

9998 = Suspense Account

Introduction

It is important to set up your opening balances correctly and in the right order. All accounts remain at zero until you enter opening balances for your Customers, Suppliers, Nominal, Bank and Products.

Where opening balances are carried forward, accurate figures need to be entered to reflect the true financial position of the business, for example, its Debtors, Creditors, Nominal Ledger Trial Balance, as well as its Stock.

Standard VAT and VAT Cash Accounting

Standard VAT calculates the VAT return on the invoices/credits you have raised for your customers or received from your suppliers, irrespective of whether they have been paid, and any bank/cash payments or receipts or journal entries with VATable tax codes.

Customer opening balances can be entered as lump sum balances. It is recommended, however, that when initially starting with Sage 50 Accounts, each outstanding invoice and credit note should be entered separately for cross-referencing. Recording separate transactions will also provide accurate aged debtor analysis.

The second method, the VAT Cash Accounting scheme, is where the VAT return is calculated on the invoices/credits which you have received payment for from your customers or you have paid to your suppliers. It also includes any bank/cash payments or receipts or journal entries with VATable tax codes.

With VAT Cash Accounting, each invoice and credit note must be entered for your customers individually, with the correct tax code.

The same Standard VAT and VAT Cash Accounting conditions apply for entering opening balances for suppliers. Again, it is recommended for Standard VAT that separate transactions be recorded for outstanding invoices and credit notes to match up with payments later, instead of grouping them all together in one opening balance. Separate transactions will again provide accurate aged creditors information.

For small businesses there is also a VAT scheme called Flat Rate. This can be invoice based or cash based. A VAT rate percentage based on your trade sector is agreed with HMRC and entered in your Company Preferences when selecting Flat Rate in the VAT scheme. Contact HMRC for further details about Flat Rate VAT.

Standard VAT – O/B

With the Standard VAT accounting method, opening balances can be entered as a lump sum or individual transactions. You set up your customer balances using the Customer Record, accessed by using the Customers option on the Sage 50 navigation bar.

Where customer information exists already, you can refer to the Aged Debtors Analysis and Detailed Customer Activity reports for cross referencing purposes, and for checking that opening balances are recorded accurately. The Aged Creditors and Detailed Supplier Activity reports are also available for your suppliers.

To enter customer Opening Balance details

1 From the Customers window click on the required record, then click the Edit button on the Customers toolbar

2 Click here to set up the Opening Balance

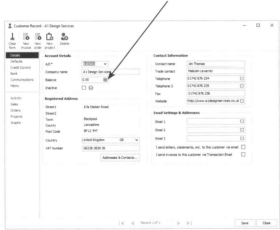

3 Enter invoice/credit note reference, the original transaction date or last date of previous financial year, Type and Gross amount

4 Click Save to record details or Cancel to discard

Hot tip

Simply follow the same procedures as for Customers when entering opening balances for your Suppliers.

Hot tip

An Opening Balance can be entered as one total amount only if a detailed breakdown is not required.

Don't forget

T9 is set as the default non-VATable tax code.

VAT Cash Accounting – O/B

Using this particular scheme each customer invoice and credit note needs entering individually with the correct tax code, because VAT is only considered when payment is being made. The opening balances can be entered using the Batch Invoices or Credits screens.

To enter customer Opening Balance details

Hot tip

To quickly identify reference numbers, use the Audit Trail from within Transactions.

1 From the Customers window click on the required record, then click the Edit button on the Customers toolbar

2 Click here to set up the Opening Balance

Hot tip

Enter the original date of the invoice or credit note for accurate aged debtors analysis or last date of the previous financial year.

148

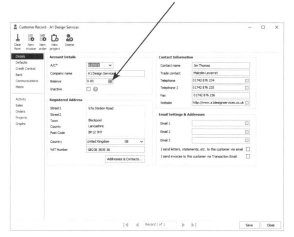

3 Enter invoice/credit note Reference, the original transaction date or last date of previous financial year and Type

4 Enter Net amount. If you want to enter a single opening balance, enter total net amount of all invoices here

Don't forget

The default tax code and VAT appear automatically, but can be changed as necessary.

5 Tax Code and VAT are entered for you. Check, then click Save

Clearing Opening Balances

When opening balances for your customers and suppliers are saved, they are posted to the Trial Balance. These entries need clearing or they will be duplicated when posting opening balances for your nominal ledger accounts. This will produce an incorrect Balance Sheet.

Before you start, make a note from your Trial Balance of the values of your Debtors and Creditors Control Accounts, your Sales Tax and Purchase Tax Control Accounts and your Suspense Account and whether each one is a debit or a credit, for example:

Trial Balance

Name	TC	Debit	Credit
Debtors Control Account	T9	30,687.19	
Creditors Control Account	T9		21,189.78
Suspense	T9		9,497.41
BALANCE		30,687.19	30,687.19

Once the relevant details have been noted, a Journal Entry from the Nominal Ledger needs to be made to clear the balances. Using the details from the above example, the entry would be as follows:

Journal Entry

Name	TC	Debit	Credit
Debtors Control Account	T9		30,687.19
Creditors Control Account	T9	21,189.78	
Suspense	T9	9,497.41	
BALANCE		30,687.19	30,687.19

Remember to print a copy of your Trial Balance Report BEFORE clearing the opening balances.

When entering Journal entries into the transaction table, use opposite values from the Trial Balance, i.e. Debit (+) and Credit (-).

The Journal entry can only be saved when the value in the Balance box is zero.

...cont'd

Once you have noted what entries you need to make, you can add them to the Journal. When you process these entries, the opening balances in the Trial Balance will be cleared. To make the entries, do the following:

1 From the menu bar, click Modules, then Nominal codes

2 Click on Journal entry from the Nominal codes window

3 The Reference entry is optional. Type a reference if desired then check for correct Posting Date

4 Enter details for both the credit and debits

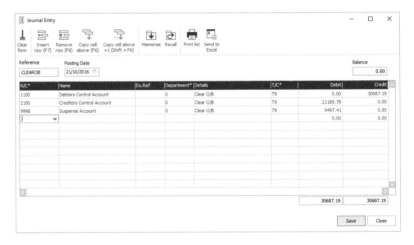

5 Note, the default Tax code of T9 is entered for you by Sage 50

6 Check total Debit and Credit are equal and a zero balance is displayed in the Balance box

7 Click Save to process your journal or Clear form to cancel

8 Click Close to return to the Nominal codes window

Beware

Always bear in mind that for a Journal entry, the VAT is neither calculated nor posted for you to the VAT control account record. You have to do this manually.

150

Hot tip

If you make a mistake just click the Clear form button and start again.

Entering Balances Mid-Year

Sage 50 needs Opening Balances in order to produce accurate financial statements. Since all accounts in all the ledgers have a zero balance when the program is first installed, it is important that the Opening Balances are entered as soon as possible. Without them, your financial statements will not be up-to-date and accurate.

It is, however, quite possible to start using Sage 50 at any time through your financial year, and then enter the Opening Balances as they become available. For instance, if you have been in business for some time, you will already have stock, products, customers and suppliers. You will have a transaction history. When you first start to use Sage 50 you will set up Records for your Customers, Suppliers, Products, etc. This is when you can start to enter some Opening Balances.

If you do start to use Sage 50 part way through your financial year, you should contact your accountant as soon as possible for a detailed list showing all your outstanding Debtors and Creditors. You can then use this as the Opening Balances for your Customers and Suppliers.

You also need to ask for a Trial Balance from your accountant, which will give you the Opening Balances for each Nominal Ledger and Bank account.

You must at all times make sure that the information you enter is accurate. If you need to enter Opening Balances part way through your financial year, you will probably have a lot of Nominal Ledger opening balances to enter as well! It is important, therefore, that you enter these accurately, otherwise your balance sheet will be incorrect.

You will also need to enter any year-to-date values from your Profit and Loss accounts. Again, your accountant should be able to provide you with this.

When you start using Sage 50 for the first time and you set up Product records, this is also a good time to have a stock take so that you know the details you are entering are accurate. Sage 50 can only produce accurate reports if the information you enter is correct. This is also the time to check that Customer and Supplier details are still up-to-date.

If you do not enter a Cost Price in the Opening Product Setup box, then the product cost is recorded as zero. This could affect your financial reports later.

Nominal Ledger & Bank A/C

When entering opening balances for your Nominal Ledger or Bank account, double-entry postings are applied by Sage 50. For example, if you post a debit opening balance of £1,000 to your Building Society account (1220 by default), Sage 50 will automatically post £1,000 as a credit to your Suspense Account (9998 by default).

After you have entered all your Nominal Ledger and Bank account opening balances, the balance of the Suspense Account should be zero again. A new Trial Balance needs to be printed to check that opening balances have been included for all your nominal accounts. If you still have a balance in your Suspense Account (i.e. it is not zero), an opening balance may have been omitted or a debit or credit misposted.

Nominal ledger opening balances

Don't forget

If you have money in the bank or building society, their statement shows you have a balance under the credit column. They owe you that money; you are the creditor. When this money is recorded in your accounts, such asset balances are recorded the opposite way round as debits. If you have money in your bank or building society, the balance must be entered as a debit.

1 From the menu bar, click Modules, then Nominal codes

2 Select the required account and click on the Edit button

3 Click the O/B button to enter the balance

Hot tip

Enter an opening balance for each nominal account that appears on your Trial Balance.

4 Enter opening balance details

5 Click Save then Close

Bank Opening Balances

You can also set up a Bank account Opening Balance directly from the Bank Record. To do this, follow these steps:

1 From the menu bar, click Modules, then Bank accounts

2 Click on the Bank account you wish to set up an Opening Balance for and click on the Edit button

3 Click the O/B button

An asset should always have a debit entry, whilst a liability should always have a credit entry.

4 Enter Date if different. Then enter the opening balance as a Receipt or Payment. If you have money in your bank, this will be a Receipt

Opening Balance Setup ✕

Ref	O/Bal
Date	21/10/2016
Receipt GBP £	1000.00
Payment GBP £	0.00

Save   Cancel

If you have money in your bank account, i.e. a debit, enter it as a Receipt. If you are overdrawn, i.e. a credit, enter it as a Payment.

5 Click Save to record the Opening balance information, then close the Bank record

Product Opening Balances

When you create a Product Record, you will probably enter an Opening Balance for that product if you already have some in stock. However, there will be times when you need to enter an Opening Balance at a later date than when the Record was first set up.

If you do the latter, when you save the Opening Balance for a product, Sage 50 posts an Adjustment In transaction, which appears on the product reports. The valuation report will show the opening stock quantity at the cost price entered. To set up a Product Opening Balance:

If you have selected the Ignore Stock Levels check box, you will not be able to enter an opening balance for that product.

1 Click Modules, then Products and services

2 Select the Product requiring an opening balance

3 Click Edit, then click O/B button on the In Stock box

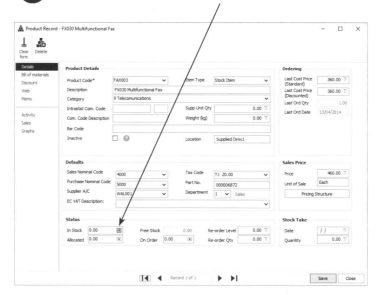

154

Hot tip

To store a JPEG image of the item with the stock record, just select the Web option then click on the Add image button on the toolbar.

4 Enter Opening Balance details here

5 Click Save to return to the Product Record, then Close

Don't forget

Remember to enter the Cost Price for the Product when you set up the Opening Balance.

14 Data Management

This chapter shows you important routines and procedures you need to use regularly to maintain your data integrity. Backing up of data is the most important, as problems could occur at any time.

Backing Up Data

Regular data backup (at least once daily) is essential in case of system error, when valuable data can be corrupted and sometimes lost. If this happens, you can at least restore important data files, reports and/or layout templates from your most up-to-date backup. A backup routine is provided by Sage 50 that remembers which drive or location you last used, but this can be changed to save to any drive and/or directory you require.

Backing up procedures vary from business to business; some use five backup media for Monday to Friday and repeat their usage the following week. The important thing is to back up your data at least once a day. Sage 50 always prompts you to back up when you exit the program, but to perform a backup at any other time, do the following:

1 From the Sage 50 menu, click on File, then Back up...

2 Click No, unless you first want to check your data

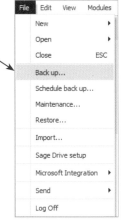

3 To back up using the default Filename, choose a Location and click OK; else to make changes follow Steps 4-5

4 To choose which File Types to back up, use the Advanced options screen

5 Click OK to start the backup

Always keep your backups in a safe and secure place.

Although you are given the option of checking your data before doing a backup, it is advisable to click No and take a backup first, just in case errors are detected and you need copies of that data. Then take a final backup, this time running the data check procedure as required.

Restoring Data

Hopefully you will not have to restore your files very often but should you be unlucky and suffer data loss or corruption, the Restore procedure allows you to revert to a previous backup. The backup you use to restore data is up to you, but it will normally be the most recent.

The Restore facility allows data from your backup media to replace your old data by erasing it and starting again. It is, therefore, very important to correctly label the media when you take a backup, and always keep it in a safe place. You may even consider keeping a second copy somewhere, other than on the premises, in case of fire or theft.

Since the restore procedure erases your old data, any data you entered after the last backup is lost and will need to be entered again, so ensure you take frequent backups. Make sure that the Restore is first necessary, then do the following:

1. From the Sage 50 menu, click on File, then Restore...

2. Click OK to restore data files from default drive, else go to Step 3

3. If you are restoring from a different drive, enter the location here

4. Click OK

5. Click OK to confirm and perform the data restore

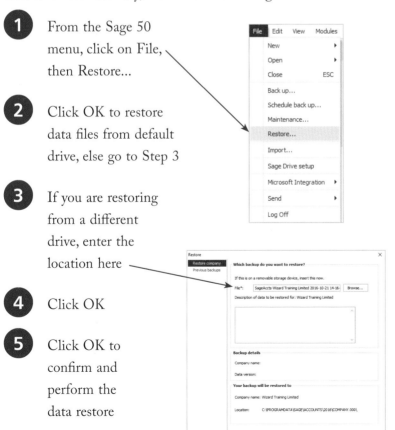

It is always advisable to run the Check Data option from File, Maintenance after you have restored your data.

Restoring data will completely erase your current Sage 50 data and replace it with data from your backup.

Changing Global Values

There are certain values in Sage 50, such as Credit Limits, that apply throughout the program. From time to time certain record values may need changing for all your records or for a selected group. To save time, these values can be changed quickly and easily by using the Global Changes Wizard. The Wizard guides you with on-screen instructions to make the necessary changes where required.

Values within the customer, supplier and nominal ledger records can be changed, as well as certain values within your product records. For example, the product sales price could be increased globally by 5% or the re-order level increased for a range of products. To run the Wizard:

Hot tip

Use the Global Changes option to alter the values for either all or for a selected group of accounts or products.

1 From the Sage 50 menu, select Tools

2 Click on Global Changes to start the Wizard, then click Next to continue

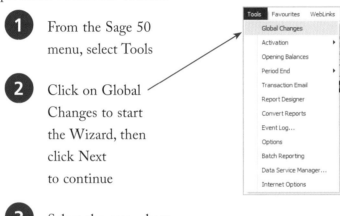

3 Select the area where you want to make a Global Change

4 Click Next to continue

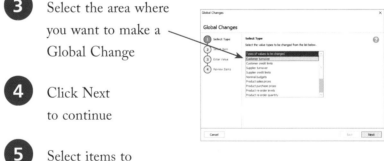

Don't forget

Remember that you can also use the Global Changes Wizard to quickly set up customer turnover and credit limits, supplier turnover and credit limits, and nominal budgets.

5 Select items to apply change to

6 Click Next to continue

7 Select type of change and enter a value before progressing

8 Click Next
to continue

9 Check correct items are to be processed

10 Check that the details are correct. If you need to make any changes, use the Back button until you get to the appropriate screen, make the changes, then keep clicking Next to get back to this screen

11 Click Post
to continue

12 Click Yes to action the changes

Whilst the Global Changes Wizard allows you to make changes quickly and easily, be very careful when using it and always double-check your values, because when you click Yes, the changes you have entered are actioned immediately. In some cases these are quite major changes, such as increasing all product sales prices by a stated percentage. If you were to accidentally enter the wrong percentage, you cannot easily undo the resulting changes!

To exit from a wizard at any point, choose the Cancel button or press Alt + F4.

Also use the Global Changes Wizard to set up Product Sales and Purchase Prices, Discount Rates, Re-order Levels and Re-order Quantities for your Products.

Always check you have entered the correct information, as you may not be able to easily undo changes.

159

Avoid import errors by not exceeding the maximum data unit length and using the correct data type, e.g. do not enter a decimal number into a integer data unit.

When importing account code data of customer and supplier records, it is converted to uppercase and restricted to eight characters. Blank spaces are removed.

Importing Data

It can be very laborious entering a lot of data into certain records, so Sage 50 lets you import data into the following record types: customers, suppliers, products and nominal ledger – provided, of course, it conforms to the correct file format. A group of new records can be created and imported directly into Sage 50 or existing records updated with new details, replacing records being entered individually.

The text can be easily produced using any program which allows you to save the file in text format (.txt), for example, a word processing, spreadsheet or accounts package. The text must be in a specific format, otherwise it will not be imported correctly and errors will be reported. These files are called CSV files (Comma Separated Values).

The following rules apply:

- A comma separates each unit of data, i.e. B01,Bolt,100,0.2.

- Each data record takes up a single line.

- Each data record is terminated by pressing ENTER.

- Any spaces at the start or end of a data unit are ignored, but spaces within data units are included.

- Use quotes to include commas within a data unit, e.g. "25, Bell Lane".

- Each data unit in a record must be entered in strict order to avoid being imported incorrectly.

- Two consecutive commas (,,) forces a move to the next data unit.

An example of three typical CSV data records:

1,SI,BROWN,4000,2,Supplies,03/10/15,,27.15,T1,Y

2,SC,WHITE,4000,2,Credit,14/10/15,,35.00,T1,N

3,PI,BLACK,5000,4,Equipment,25/11/15,,52.50,T1,Y

To Import a Data File

1 From the Sage 50 menu, select File, then click Import...

2 Click Next then select Data Type here

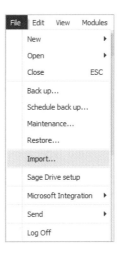

3 Click Next to continue

4 Select import format and click on the Browse button

5 Enter Name of File to Import or select from the list

6 Click Open then Next, Next again, then Finish

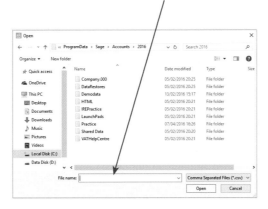

The inclusion of a SPACE between two commas (, ,) causes the existing data to be erased.

Importing a blank unit of data does not overwrite existing data – it simply leaves it intact and forces a move to the next data unit. Use this feature for changing only selected data in a record.

A list of file import details is available from the Help facility for customer and supplier records, nominal ledger audit trail transactions, stock records and all stock transactions.

File Maintenance

Sage 50 provides five important options to manage and check the validity of your data files. These features involve checking for input errors, recovery tools for repairing the integrity of your data, data compression, re-indexing and building new data files.

Error Checking

You should use the Check Data facility to check the validity of your data files. If necessary you can then make corrections where required. This facility needs to be run regularly, when making backups and after restoring data.

Hot tip

Use the Check Data option on a regular basis to check for errors, so they can be quickly detected and rectified.

Don't forget

If there are problems whilst checking the data, a File Maintenance Problem Report dialog box appears which includes a Summary and details of Comments, Errors or Warnings.

Hot tip

To print out an error report, select the required report category from the File Maintenance Problems Report dialog box and click the Print button.

162

1. From the Sage 50 menu, select File, then click on Maintenance

2. From the File maintenance window click Check Data

3. Checking Data Files box shows the progress

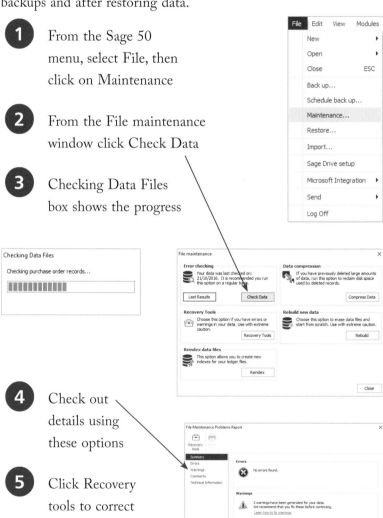

4. Check out details using these options

5. Click Recovery tools to correct errors, else click Close to finish

Recovery Tools

Sometimes errors are due to a corruption that has disrupted the integrity of the data files. This can often be corrected using the various Recovery Tools facilities. For example, to recover from transaction errors, do the following:

1 To recover the transaction history, click on Recalculate Transaction History from the Recovery Tools window

2 Recalculation progress displays

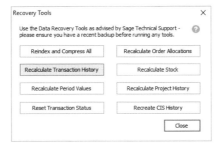

3 Click OK when finished

4 To repair transaction status, click Reset Transaction Status from the Recovery Tools window

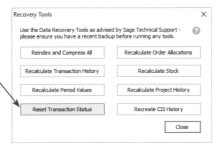

5 Click OK when transaction resetting is complete

Reset Transaction Status checks for any unallocated transactions which should be allocated. If any are found it changes the transaction type – SR becomes SA, PP becomes PA, SD becomes SC and PD becomes PC.

Use the recovery tools with caution. If in doubt, seek advice from Sage Technical Support first. For contact details refer to the Weblinks or Help options on the Sage menu.

If you suspect there has been data corruption, try using Reindex to create new indexes for your ledger files.

...cont'd

Data Compression

When there has been a lot of activity, such as deletion or amendments of any records, use the Compress Data option to produce a new set of data files. Sage 50 will then reduce file size by removing these deleted records, freeing up disk space. To perform data compression, do this:

You can choose to compress all data files or only selected ones.

1 Click Compress Data from the File maintenance window

2 Click Compress

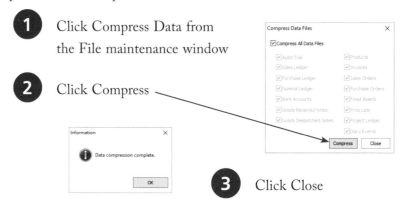

3 Click Close

Rebuild

This Sage 50 option is for creating a new or selected set of data files. From the File maintenance window:

1 Click Rebuild

2 Select files to keep, and click OK

3 Click Yes to confirm

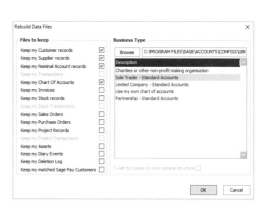

4 Check Financial Year and click OK, then Yes

5 Click OK to finish

Take care when using the Rebuild option as it will clear the contents of your existing data files. USE WITH CAUTION.

Write Off, Refund & Return

Use these options to carry out accounting procedures that affect your customer and supplier accounts, e.g. cheque returns, invoice refunds and outstanding invoice transactions. The way you record these depends on your VAT method.

Refunds

Use this facility for credit notes, payments on account and invoices where a money refund is required rather than a replacement of goods or provision of services. If you are using the Standard VAT Scheme, do the following:

1 From the Suppliers toolbar click on the Write offs & returns button

2 Select where you want to make the amendments

3 Click here

4 Select the account to which the invoice refund is to be made

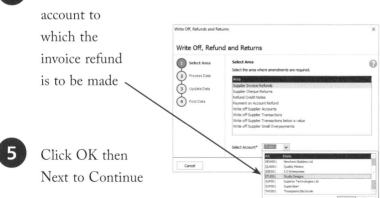

5 Click OK then Next to Continue

Don't forget

Sage 50 procedures for these functions vary depending on whether you are using the Standard VAT Scheme or VAT Cash Accounting.

Hot tip

For VAT Cash Accounting the transaction needs writing off manually. For more information, refer to the Recording Refunds (VAT Cash Accounting) section of the Sage Help.

Hot tip

To find out if you are able to reclaim VAT paid on a Write Off, call HM Revenue and Customs.

...cont'd

Remember that this option is NOT suitable for anyone using VAT Cash Accounting as it does not adjust the VAT value for you.

6 Select the invoice being refunded

7 Click Clear to make the correction

8 Select the bank account you wish to post to

9 Click OK and Next

10 Enter the correct date to use for the transaction

11 Click Next

12 A summary now appears

If the presented summary of information is incorrect, simply use the Back button to return to the appropriate box and modify.

13 Check carefully that it is all correct. Use the Back button if you need to make any changes, else go to Step 14

14 Click Post to post changes to your ledgers

...cont'd

Write Off

At times, a customer will not or cannot pay an outstanding debt, so the amount has to be written off to a bad debt account. The steps are very similar to a Refund, but fewer. Just select the appropriate Write Off for Step 2 on page 165 and follow the simple instructions.

Cheque Returns

Occasionally, you may need to record a cheque from a customer that you wish to cancel or that the bank has returned. If you use the Standard VAT Scheme, do this:

1 From the Customers toolbar, click on the Write offs & returns button

2 Click Customer Cheque Returns

Write offs & returns

3 Select account, and click Next

4 Select the cheque, click Next then carry out Steps 10-14 on page 166

Using a credit note to refund an outstanding customer invoice is known as allocating the credit note to the customer invoice.

When a sales credit note is posted to the customer's account it assumes the same reference as the refunded invoice.

To record a refund using the Write Off, Refunds and Returns Wizard, the refund must need to be fully refunded and must not have been removed from the Audit Trail. If it has been removed or you need to make a partial refund, you must use the manual refund method.

Posting Contra Entries

Where you have a customer who is also one of your suppliers, you may offset sales invoices against your supplier's purchase invoices. Use the Contra Entries option from within Customers or Suppliers to match one or more sales invoices with your purchase invoices. Sage 50 will then automatically update the appropriate ledgers. To post a Contra Entry:

Don't forget

If VAT Cash Accounting is being used, make sure the selected transactions have matching tax codes.

1 From the Sage 50 navigation bar, select Customers or Suppliers

2 Click on the Contra entries button in the toolbar to bring up the Contra Entries window

Contra entries

3 Select Customer (Sales Ledger) and Supplier (Purchase Ledger) accounts

Don't forget

You cannot amend any of the values shown in the Total boxes.

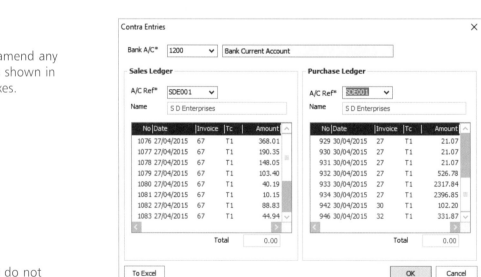

	Contra Entries				✕

Bank A/C* `1200` `Bank Current Account`

Sales Ledger

A/C Ref* `SDE001`
Name `S D Enterprises`

No	Date	Invoice	Tc	Amount
1076	27/04/2015	67	T1	368.01
1077	27/04/2015	67	T1	190.35
1078	27/04/2015	67	T1	148.05
1079	27/04/2015	67	T1	103.40
1080	27/04/2015	67	T1	40.19
1081	27/04/2015	67	T1	10.15
1082	27/04/2015	67	T1	88.83
1083	27/04/2015	67	T1	44.94

Total `0.00`

Purchase Ledger

A/C Ref* `SDE001`
Name `S D Enterprises`

No	Date	Invoice	Tc	Amount
929	30/04/2015	27	T1	21.07
930	30/04/2015	27	T1	21.07
931	30/04/2015	27	T1	21.07
932	30/04/2015	27	T1	526.78
933	30/04/2015	27	T1	2317.84
934	30/04/2015	27	T1	2396.85
942	30/04/2015	30	T1	102.20
946	30/04/2015	32	T1	331.87

Total `0.00`

To Excel   OK   Cancel

Hot tip

If your totals do not match, a warning message appears asking whether you want to make part-Contra Entries for the lowest amount. If acceptable, click the Yes button or No to cancel the Contra Entries.

4 Select outstanding invoice (on Sales side) from the list

5 Select invoice to apply Contra Entry for

6 Click OK to finish

Run Period End Functions

Period End options are essential monthly and year end procedures for updating the accounting system. For example, for posting accruals, prepayments and depreciation. The Audit Trail can then be cleared of any unwanted transactions, whilst stock can be cleared from your product history if you so wish.

Through running these procedures, you will also be preparing Sage 50 so that it is ready for you to enter transactions when moving into a new financial period.

Month End

At each month end it is important to post your prepayments, accruals and depreciation values. Sage 50 will process these transactions automatically and update your nominal account records and Audit Trail for you. The option also exists to clear down your month-to-date turnover figures for your customer and supplier records.

Once you have run the Month End procedure, this is an opportune time to produce some of your financial reports, for example, the Profit and Loss, Balance Sheet, Trial Balance, Budget and Prior Year Analysis reports. Customer statements and Aged Analysis reports for Debtors and Creditors will also prove useful.

Month End Guidelines

Here is a check list for the Month End:

- Check all relevant transactions have been posted

- Check recurring entries have been set up and processed

- Check prepayments, accruals and depreciation have been set up

- Complete your bank reconciliation

- Print product history, valuation and profit reports

- Post product Journals for your Profit and Loss and Balance Sheet

If the Program Date needs changing for Month End procedure, select Change Program Date from the Settings menu. Remember to re-set the date back to the correct date when done.

Back up your data files before and after running Month End procedures.

Use File Maintenance Check and Compress Data options to check your files.

...cont'd

Hot tip

If you have multicompany Sage 50, you can use the Consolidation option from Period End to merge the data from your separate companies to form one set of financial accounts.

After following the Month End guidelines it is time to run the Month End procedure. You will probably want to run it on a day other than the actual last calendar day of the month, as this is often more convenient. You will therefore have to change the program date first. To do this, simply follow these steps:

1 First, back up your data files

2 From the Sage 50 menu bar, click Settings

3 Click on Change Program Date...

4 Enter the last day of the month

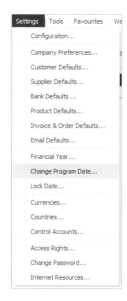

5 Click OK

6 From the Sage 50 menu, click on Tools

7 Select Period End

8 Click on Month End

9 In the Month End window, use Check Data to check for errors, then the Backup button to first back up your data

10 Select the required options in the Month End Options area, enter or change any dates if necessary, then click Run Month End button to run the procedure

Year End

Before you run the Year End, Month End procedures must be completed, together with any final adjustments.

First, when you run Month End on the last month of the current financial year, DO NOT clear the Audit Trail. Once values for the Month End have been checked and you are satisfied that they are correct, set the program date to the last date of the current financial year and run Year End:

1 Set the program date to the last day of the financial year by doing Steps 1-5 on page 170

2 From the Sage 50 menu, click on Tools

3 Select Period End

4 Click on Year End

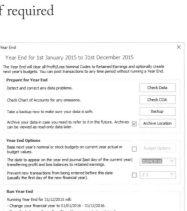

5 Check data then take a backup using the buttons provided, tick to Archive if required

6 Tick to update budget figures if required

7 Correct Year End Journal Date if necessary

8 Click Run Year End to complete process

Lastly, remove any unwanted Customer, Supplier, Nominal, Bank and Product records and reset system date. You are now ready to continue entering transactions for the new financial year.

Hot tip

Take at least two backups of your data files, both before and after running the Year End routine.

Beware

After Year End, check your Financial Year Start Date before entering any new transactions.

Beware

You must not consolidate companies that have different base currencies.

171

Clearing Audit Trail & Stock

This option lets you remove paid and reconciled transactions prior to a specified date from the Audit Trail. This makes the ledgers easier to read. Reconciled transactions on the nominal ledger are brought forward as opening balances.

Sage 50 can store up to 2,000,000,000 transactions in the Audit Trail, so transactions do not have to be removed, but by deleting unwanted transactions it will free disk space and provide faster access to information.

Don't forget

Only paid, allocated and reconciled transactions are removed from the Audit Trail.

1 From the Tools menu, select Period End, click Clear audit trail, then enter required date

2 Click Clear audit trail to start the process, and enter details in the next screen for taking a backup

3 Click OK to back up, then OK again when finished

Don't forget

Before running the Clear Stock option, you should back up your data and print your stock valuation and stock history reports. Do likewise before clearing the Audit Trail.

Clear Stock

This option can be run as part of the Month End and Year End procedures. It allows you to decide when to clear transactions from your Product History.

1 From the Tools menu, select Period End and Clear Stock

2 Choose to clear all stock records or just those selected and check date

Beware

Departmental reporting and activity will be affected by removing transactions from the Audit Trail.

3 Click Clear stock

4 Click OK when finished

15 Task Management

Here, you are shown how to use the Diary module for recording meetings or appointment reminders, people to contact, etc. After reviewing your debtors you can record promised payments and even when to pay your own bills.

Features of the Diary Module

The Diary module makes it easy for you to manage your time and the tasks you need to do. Use the Diary to set up a list of jobs and to prompt you of any that are currently due, overdue or recently completed. By setting up these tasks, it acts as a reminder of the actions you need to take to run your business efficiently, helps you liaise with your debtors and saves valuable time.

You can use the Diary to help you:

- Set up a list of tasks that you need to do and also view tasks that are either completed, due or overdue.

- List who you need to contact today or in the future. You can then log any calls you make to customers whilst chasing payment, together with the outcome.

- Review bills that are due for payment or overdue.

- Check when you have promised to pay your suppliers and, more importantly, set up reminders of when your customers have promised to pay you.

- Keep on top of the payment activity of your customers. For example, you will be able to see at a glance when overdue accounts were followed up and when payment was promised by.

- Quickly check for any disputes you may have recorded between yourself and your customers or suppliers, with an easy to read view of the details and reason.

- Keep track of when you can make payments to suppliers. You can quickly manage all payments due from the Suppliers module, including how much you can afford to pay at that time. Let Sage 50 suggest payments to creditors and if you have enough money in the bank to do so, record all of this in the Diary so that you will receive reminders when the time comes to make these payments.

You can also import appointments from Microsoft Outlook into the Diary as well as export Diary events and contacts back into Microsoft Outlook.

Hot tip

To clear an event from the To-do list, simply highlight it and click on the Delete button.

Hot tip

Event types are colour coded for you to make them easy to identify.

The Diary Window

The Diary window has a similar layout to the other Sage 50 modules, with a toolbar above the Diary view area. The toolbar buttons are used to change the Diary view, as follows:

Day

To Display the Diary in Day View

Work week

To Display the Diary in Work Week View

Week

To Display the Diary in Week View

Month

To Display the Diary in Month View

⦿To-do list To Switch to the To-do List View

⦿Diary   To Switch to the Diary View

175

To bring up the Diary window, do the following:

1 On the Sage 50 navigation bar, click Diary

2 When the Diary appears, select the view you require

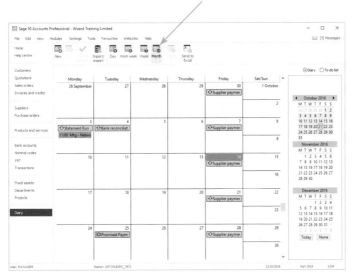

Setting Up a Diary Task

Use the Diary (or To-do list option) to create a list of tasks you need to complete. The types of tasks include a general reminder, a meeting or appointment, contact a customer, overdue letters, print management reports, etc. Any additional information that may prove useful can be entered in the Notes box.

Once saved, the task appears on the Diary day and in the To-do list. The Diary/To-do list can then be viewed at any time. To set up a Diary task, proceed as follows:

Hot tip

To create a new event and have Sage enter the start date and time for you, simply double-click on the appropriate section of the Diary day.

1 Open the Diary and select the appropriate Diary view

2 Select required day and click New button on the toolbar

3 Enter Subject, Location and Type from the drop-down list

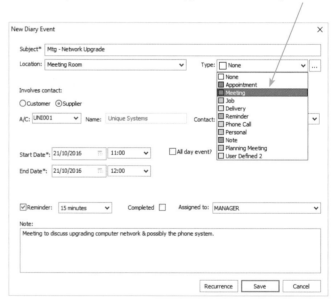

4 Complete the Contact details, Time and Date

5 Set a Reminder. Sage will then inform you when it is due

6 Type the appropriate details in the Note area

7 Click Save for the event to appear in the Diary view

Hot tip

If you don't wish to be reminded when an event is due, simply remove the Reminder tick.

Setting Up a Recurring Event

The Diary also allows you to set up a recurring event, such as a regular weekly management meeting, or even a personal event, like an after work session at the gym, for example.

1 Select the Day view and click on time required

2 Right-click the time and select Add

3 Enter Subject, Location and Type from the drop-down list

4 Complete the Contact details, Time and Date

5 Set a Reminder and enter details in the Note area

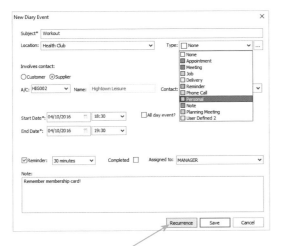

6 Click Recurrence

7 Check details are correct and amend if necessary

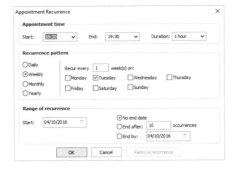

8 Click OK, then Save

9 Switch to Month view and note that a recurring weekly Diary event has been created for you

Don't forget

When exporting events to Outlook, all instances of a recurring entry will be exported, irrespective of the date range you have chosen.

Hot tip

If you make a mistake when setting up a new event, simply click Cancel and start again.

Don't forget

When you have created a recurring entry, always check the Diary to see if any future events fall on days when they cannot take place, e.g. on a bank holiday.

177

Completing an Event

To Snooze a Reminder

When you have set a Reminder, Sage brings up a window at the appropriate time to prompt you of the approaching event. You can dismiss the reminder or, if there is still more than 15 minutes to go, ask Sage to remind you again nearer the time, as follows:

1 Select the event you wish to be reminded of again later

2 Select how soon you want to be reminded again

3 Click Snooze

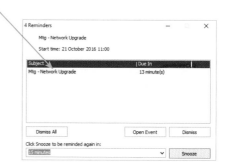

Don't forget

Depending on how much time there is before the event takes place, the Snooze option may not be available.

To mark an event as Completed

Once an event has taken place, you can either delete it or keep it in the Diary for reference and simply mark it as completed.

1 From the Diary view or To-do list, double-click on the required event to open the event window

2 Click the Completed box

3 Click Save (Reminder tick will be removed automatically)

Don't forget

You don't need to remove the Reminder tick when marking an event as completed. The Diary does this for you when you click Save.

Chasing Debt

You can use the Diary to follow up a promised payment. On the promised date a Sage Diary reminder will then prompt you to check that payment has been received, thus allowing you to keep a close track of your debtors. The promise is set up in Customers.

To create an automated Promised Payment event

1 Just below the toolbar in the top right-hand corner of the Customers window, select Chase debt

2 Double-click on a customer with a high overdue balance and click Communications in the navigation bar

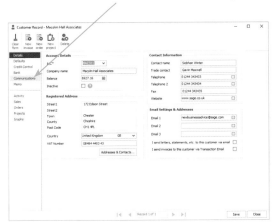

3 In the Communications window, click on Add entry button

Whenever the Customer record is called up, Sage will remind you if the account is on hold or terms not agreed, etc.

Use the previous and next buttons to quickly switch between Customers, if more than one has been selected.

179

Remember to ensure that a filter is not applied, otherwise all debtors may not be listed.

...cont'd

Quickly print out a list of customers On Hold or customers Over Credit Limit using the Chase Debt Reports function.

4 Contact the customer to discuss how they propose to settle their account. Record the telephone conversation duration with the Telephone Timer, the details of who you spoke to in the Contact Details section, and in the Communication Result section record the details of the payment promised

5 Click Save, then Save again

6 Close the Customer record and the Customers window

7 The promised date is now highlighted in the Calendar and an event shown at the top of the Diary for that day

Managing Payments

You can also use the Diary to record and remind you when you need to pay your Suppliers.

1 In the top right-hand corner of the Suppliers window, select Manage payments

⦿Manage payments

2 Click the Suggest payments button on the toolbar

3 A window appears showing what you owe suppliers

4 Enter Funds for Payment here and select a bank account

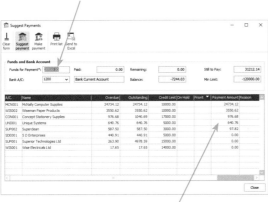

5 Clicking Suggest payment shows recommended payments. To pay, click Make payment button and follow the steps on page 62, or enter payment details in Supplier record as per promised payments (page 179-180) to receive Diary reminders

Hot tip

For a printout of all the Suppliers you owe money to, just click the Print list button.

181

Don't forget

If you leave the Funds for Payment box blank, Sage checks the balance and minimum limit of the bank account you have chosen, to see what funds are available, and makes a suitable recommendation.

Office Integration

The Sage 50 Diary integrates with Microsoft Outlook. Contacts and events set up in the Diary can be exported to Outlook, whilst appointments can be imported from Outlook into the Diary.

To Import appointments

A handy process helps you easily import events from Outlook:

Beware

You can only import or export events from or to Microsoft Outlook.

1 From the Diary toolbar click the Import/export button

2 Click Yes to bring up the Select Action screen

3 Select Import Outlook Diary Events and click Next

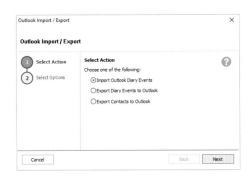

4 Enter a date range for the Outlook events you wish to import

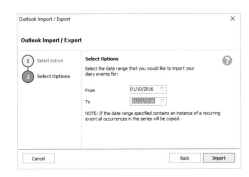

Don't forget

The Diary can only provide accurate debt management information if correct data has been entered in the first place. Therefore, always make full use of the Customer and Supplier details recording facilities.

5 Always check your choice of dates is correct and then click Import to start the process

6 Answer any prompts as necessary to complete the import

Note that imported events have a label of None in the Diary. If you wish you can then edit the entry to show a suitable label.

To Export appointments

The handy process is also used to quickly take you through the
steps for exporting your Sage Diary events to Microsoft Outlook,
as follows:

1 From the Diary toolbar click the
Import/export button

2 Click Yes to bring up the Select Action screen

Hot tip

Save time by using the
Send to Excel button to
send the contents of a
list directly to Excel.

Send to
Excel

3 Select Export
Diary Events
to Outlook and
click Next

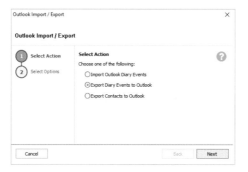

4 Enter a date
range for the
Diary events
you wish
to export

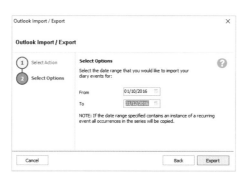

Hot tip

If you make a mistake,
simply click Back, or
Cancel and start again.

5 Always check your choice of dates is correct and
then click Export to start the process

6 Answer any prompts as necessary to complete the export

Note that as with imported events, exported events have a label of
None in Outlook. Again, you can then edit the entry in Outlook
to show a suitable label.

...cont'd

To Export Diary Contacts

The third function of the Sage 50 Import/Export Wizard is to quickly help you export your Sage Diary contacts to Microsoft Outlook, as follows:

Before exporting contact details to Outlook, make sure the information is accurate and complete.

1 From the Diary toolbar click the Import/export button

2 Click Yes to bring up the Select Action screen

3 Select Export Contacts to Outlook and click Next

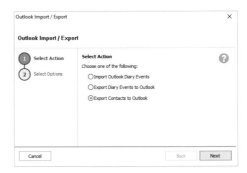

4 Select the Ledgers you wish to export the Diary contacts for

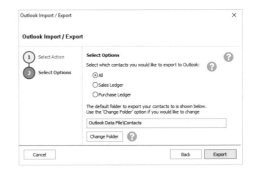

Importing or Exporting normally only fails if the correct User Profile has not been selected or set up in Outlook.

5 Check your choice, use the Back button if you have made a mistake, else click Export to start the process

6 Answer any prompts as necessary to complete the export of contacts from Sage to Outlook

If there is a problem during the export, you are returned to Step 4. Click on Change Folder and find the correct Outlook folder.

User Defined Labels

When creating a new Diary event, Sage provides you with a handy drop-down list of pre-defined event types to choose from.

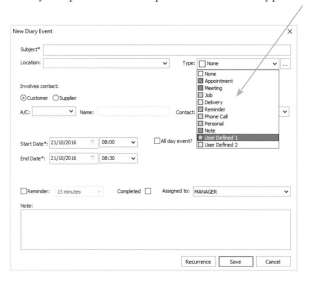

Hot tip

To show an event as lasting all day, just click the All day event box.

However, the last two in the list are reserved for the user to define as follows:

1 Select the appropriate Diary view

2 Right-click the day required and select Add

3 Enter a Subject and Location

4 Click here, to the right of the Type box

5 Type a name for either the first, or both, labels

6 Click OK, then choose your new label and click Save

Don't forget

When you place a tick in the All day event box, the start and end time entry boxes become hidden, and vice versa.

Managing Events

To View events

Use the To-do list view to quickly see Diary events already set up.

1 From the top right of the Diary window, select To-do list

2 Choose the required Diary view, e.g. Month

3 All events for that period are displayed

Hot tip

Just click on the day line in the Calendar grid (the dark area just under the day date) and start typing to add a quick diary note.

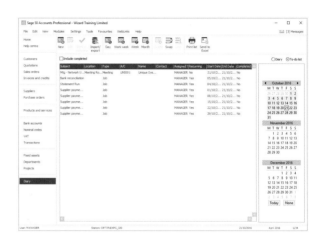

To Delete an event

You would normally leave events in the Diary for reference. To delete an event, however, such as a cancelled meeting:

1 From the top right of the Diary window, select To-do list and choose the required day, week or month view

2 Select the event or task you want to delete

3 Click the Delete button

Hot tip

To quickly reschedule an appointment or meeting, simply drag it to the new day and timeline. The details are amended automatically for you.

Index

D

E

F

G

H

I

J

L

M

Q

R

S

T

U

V

W

Y